THE AWAKENING GLOSSARY
THE LANGUAGE OF THE BEAUTIFUL GOSPEL

Greek Terms & Key Scriptures from AWAKENING: Restorative Metanoia

THE AWAKENING GLOSSARY
THE LANGUAGE OF THE BEAUTIFUL GOSPEL

Greek Terms & Key Scriptures from
AWAKENING: Restorative Metanoia

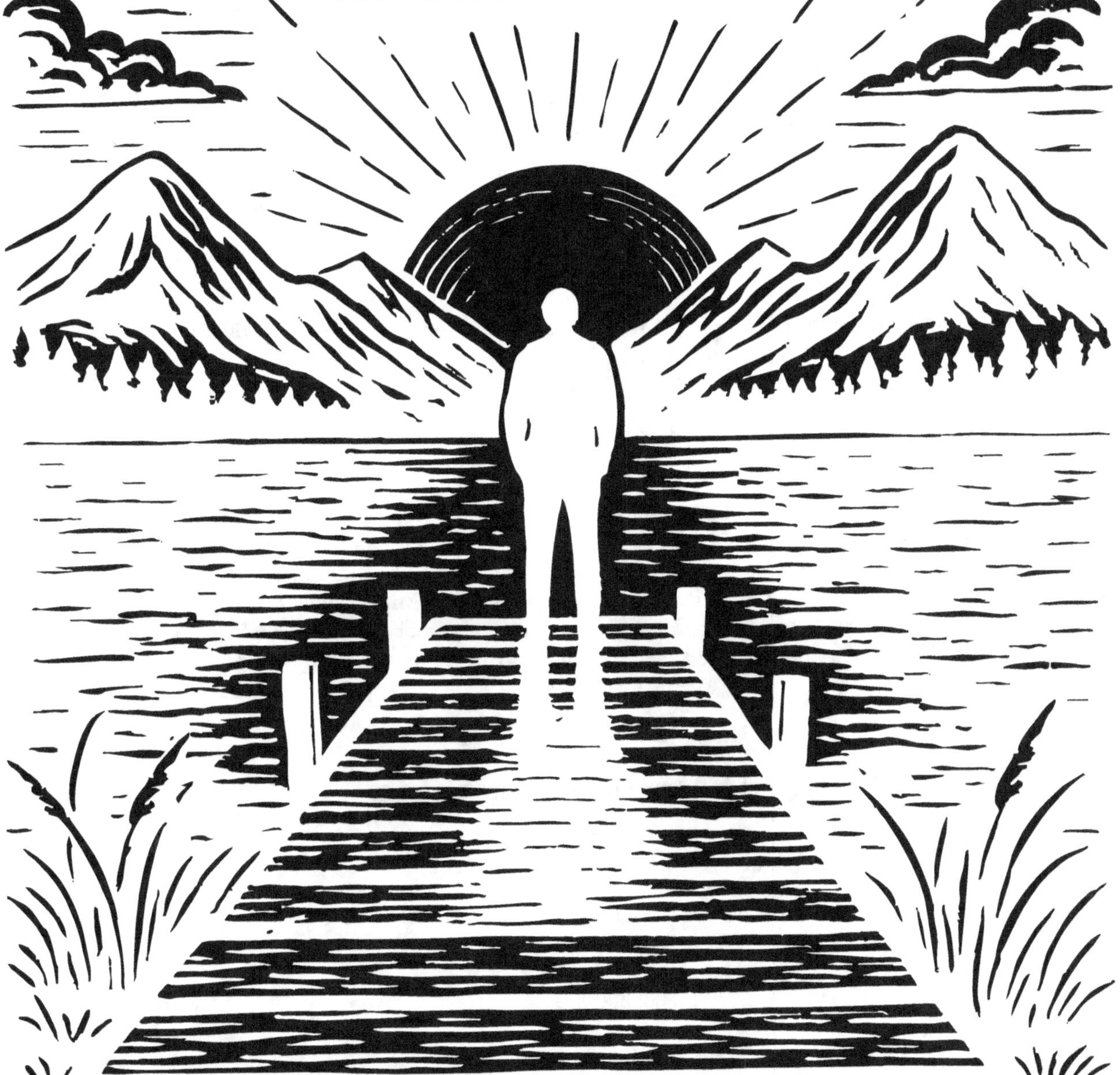

BRYAN ELLIOTT

Spirit Media Publishing

Foreword

Page after page of this remarkable work unfolds the mystery of the greatest discovery in the universe — holding a looking glass over sentences and words which echo within us from a deeper place than surface and time-bound perceptions. "Revealing the breathtaking truth that you were never outside God's love, only temporarily blind to your eternal inclusion in His embrace."

I find myself often in tears of joy at the profound yet simple urging to awaken to the freshness of the new day that has dawned.

Bryan highlights one of the most misunderstood yet most vital words in Bible vocabulary — the Greek word metanoia, sadly translated again and again as "repentance."

Metanoia comes from meta, together with, and noeō, to perceive with the mind. It describes the awakening of the mind to that which is true — a re-alignment of one's reasoning, a co-knowing. It has nothing in common with the Latin word paenitentia, where the word penance stems from — meaning payback and punishment inflicted on oneself. This gross deception led to centuries of guilt-driven religion. The business of religion desperately needs paying and returning customers. The entire system was challenged and condemned by Jesus.

Isaiah 55 gives meaning to metanoia: your thoughts were distanced from God's thoughts as the heavens are from the earth — but just as rain cancels that distance and saturates the soil, so shall His word be. Metanoia suggests a co-knowing with God. An intertwining of thought. To agree with God about me.

This compact glossary carries that same revelation in portable form. The One who knew you before you were formed, who has always unconditionally and relentlessly loved you — He now hovers over your innermost being in anticipation of the closest possible intimate union you were designed and destined for.

This is not to be read in a rush. It is a work of divine proportions.

— Francois du Toit Author, The Mirror Study Bible

CONTENTS

This glossary is the companion resource to Awakening: Restorative Metanoia by Bryan Elliott. It is also designed to stand alone as a condensed reference—a transformation tool you can return to daily, whether or not you have read the full book.

INTRODUCTION

A NOTE ON SOURCES

UNDERSTANDING THE TWO DIAGRAMS

QUICK REFERENCE

THE ESSENTIAL AWAKENING GLOSSARY

Section 1: The Most Essential Terms — 31

APPENDIX

CLOSING

The Language of Awakening

**Everything Bryan Elliott produces is free at M46Ministries.com.
What God gives freely, we share freely.**

"In him, all the fullness of Deity resides in a human body. He proves that human life is tailor-made for God. And since we are in him — by design and redemption — there is no shortfall in us. Jesus mirrors our completeness and endorses our true identity. He is 'I am' in us."
— Colossians 2:9-10 (Mirror Study Bible)

Hearing stirs the faith of Christ within you.

His goodness restores.

Love was always the reality...

You Were Never the Defendant

Before the foundation of the world, the Father chose you in Christ — not because of what you would do, but because of who He is (Ephesians 1:4). The Father gave all judgment to Jesus (John 5:22) — the same Jesus who declared His entire mission in a single line: "The Son of Man came to seek and to save the lost" (Luke 19:10 NIV). The judge is the seeker. The one with all authority used it not to condemn but to find.

Then John the Baptist saw Jesus coming and declared: "Look, the Lamb of God, who takes away the sin of the world!" (John 1:29 NIV). Not covers. Not manages conditionally. Takes away. For the world. The greatest prophet who ever lived pointed at Jesus and announced a scope that religion has been quietly shrinking ever since.

And before the cross — before the resurrection, before Pentecost, before anyone had "accepted" anything — Jesus looked at the people around Him and said: "The Kingdom of God is within you" (Luke 17:21 NIV). Not coming one day. Not available after a decision. Within you. Already. Now. The union was never a transaction. It was always a reality awaiting recognition.

And then the work was finished. "God was reconciling the world to himself in Christ, not counting people's sins against them" (2 Corinthians 5:19 NIV). Not will reconcile. Not might reconcile. Was reconciling. Past tense. Already accomplished. Not counting.

Jesus said: "You will know the truth, and the truth will set you free" (John 8:32 NIV). The Greek word for truth — aletheia — doesn't mean correct information to defend. It means unveiled reality. The veil being lifted. What was always there, finally seen. This is what every scripture above has been doing — not adding something new, but removing what obscured what was always true. Freedom isn't the destination. It's what happens when the fog lifts.

You were never the defendant. You were always the one being sought. And the case was closed before you knew there was one.

We began in Christ. We are awakening to a union that was never broken.

This is *awakening.*

And yet — a gift unacknowledged remains unopened. The door is wide open. You must walk through it. Jesus is the way — the only way. The gift is universal in scope. It is not automatic in application.

The One Word That Bridges Everything

There is one word that bridges everything in these pages from truth you know to truth you live: yielding. Not striving harder. Not understanding more. Not performing better. Simply — yielding. Opening the hand. Releasing what you've been carrying. Saying yes to what God has already said yes to. This was the beginning of this journey for me — not a dramatic moment, not a theological breakthrough, but a quiet act of surrender in 2016 that changed everything. I stopped trying to produce what only He could give. And from that place of yielding, the awakening began to unfold. That's not a coincidence. Resurrection power — the same energy that raised Christ from the dead — is already at work in you (Philippians 2:13). It doesn't need your performance. It only needs your permission. Yield — and watch what He does.

Every awakening has a language.

Not a religious language — not more theology to memorize or doctrine to defend. But a living vocabulary that reshapes how you read Scripture, how you hear God, and how you see yourself. When you learn this language, something accelerates. The fog lifts faster. The truth lands deeper. What once required years of striving begins to simply settle.

That's what this guide is. The language of awakening — compact, portable, yours to carry with you.

Bring it to your small group and learn the language together. Hand it out at a conference as a free resource that opens doors. Keep it on your nightstand and reach for it when old patterns of thinking try to reassert themselves. This isn't a textbook to complete — it's a vocabulary to inhabit.

If you've been a Christian for years and still feel like you're not quite enough — still striving, still anxious, still measuring the distance between who you are and who you think God needs you to be — this language is for you.

What Is Awakening?

But first — what is awakening, exactly? Not a new spiritual movement. Not a departure from Christianity. It is the oldest thing in it. Awakening is the moment the fog of sin-consciousness lifts and you see what Scripture has been saying all along: that you are already in Christ, already complete, already held in an inseparable union you did nothing to earn and can do nothing to lose. Not becoming something new — remembering what you have always been. The Greek word at the heart of it — metanoia, translated "repentance" in most Bibles — doesn't mean guilt-driven sorrow or behavioral reform. It means the transformation of perception. Sight restored. That's awakening. And once you see it, you cannot unsee it.

It was there all along. In 400 AD, Jerome translated the Greek word metanoia — transformation of

perception — into the Latin paenitentia. Penance. Sorrow. Try harder. That single choice shaped sixteen centuries of Western Christianity. The Eastern Church, still reading Greek, never lost the original. We're not inventing something new. We're recovering something ancient.

What Awakening Restores

And what awakens us? Not fear. Not guilt. Not the threat of what happens if we don't. Romans 2:4 tells us plainly — it is the kindness of God that leads to metanoia. His goodness is the engine of awakening. Before you were born, before you could succeed or fail, before the foundation of the world — you were chosen, loved, accepted, and known. Not known as you will be one day. Known as you are, right now, exactly as you have always been known. Safe. Secure. Cherished. The awakening isn't God deciding to love you. It's you finally believing He always has.

And when you finally believe it — not as doctrine but as lived reality — the distance collapses. Intimacy becomes possible. Not earned. Not performed. Simply received.

And what awakening restores, more than anything else, is intimacy. A heart that doesn't feel safe doesn't draw close — it performs. It earns. It manages sin carefully, not because it loves God, but because it's trying to maintain a standing it was never sure it had. This is the loop religion hands you: live in sin-consciousness — perpetually aware of the gap between who you are and who God needs you to be — perform to earn love, manage sin to preserve your standing, and call the whole exhausting cycle faithfulness. But underneath it all runs the illusion of separation — the lie that God's love is still pending, still conditional, still waiting on your next move. It isn't. It never was. Awakening is the shift from sin-consciousness to righteousness-consciousness — from measuring the distance to discovering there is none. The Greek word parresia — translated "boldness" in most Bibles — means the freedom of speech that belongs to a child who knows they are safe, loved, and fully accepted — not because of what they've done but because of whose they are. No rehearsed words. No fear of rejection. No sin to manage before you can draw close. Just the unguarded access of someone who has come home. That's what awakening restores. Not just right theology. The closeness you were always made for.

Tied to all of this is the religious misreading of dying to self. Religion turned it into a daily programme of self-destruction — suppress yourself, deny yourself, diminish yourself — as though God requires your continuous crucifixion to draw close to Him. But Paul tells a different story entirely. In over 160 references across his letters, he returns again and again to the same phrase: in Christ. Not toward Christ. Not working for Christ. Not hoping to reach Christ. In Him. Already. Now. That is your address — fixed, permanent, established by resurrection. And from that address, Paul declares: you were co-crucified with Christ — past tense, completed, done to you, not by you. Co-buried. Co-resurrected. Co-seated in heavenly places. The self that died was never your true self — it was the false self, the sin-conscious, performance-driven, orphan-thinking version that was never who God saw when He looked at you. What rose is the real you — hidden in Christ, complete in Him, bearing His image from the beginning. When you know the truth of your identity, your

standing, and that God is not just loving but IS love — everything changes. You stop dying to get close. You live from the closeness that the resurrection already secured.

One Man's Journey — Documented

I never set out to write an awakening series. That's not what I planned. But that is what emerged — book by book, revelation by revelation. Looking back, I can see it clearly: the series itself is the process of metanoia in real time. Not learning something new. Remembering. Like the Kingdom, awakening doesn't announce itself. It simply unfolds from within — from the heart to the head, not the other way around.

This glossary is a companion to The Awakening Series. But that series isn't a theological curriculum — it's a journey. One man being led step by step, out of religion and into the heart of God. Every book is a documented stage of that journey.

At its core, The Awakening Series is one thing: a continued revelation of the infinite goodness of God. Not a theology of fear. Not a system to master. An ever-deepening discovery that God is infinitely better than religion described — and that it keeps getting better.

If you're reading this and you're still in the traditional gospel — the gospel of sin management, behaviour modification, and trying to be good enough — you are exactly where this journey begins. That's not a criticism. It's where all of us start. It's where this journey started too.

More Than Gold — The traditional gospel — it's where all of us start. Solid foundation, real faith. But there is more.

As in Heaven: Living in God's Kingdom Now — The Lord opens a revelation: the Kingdom isn't future or far away. It's present reality — available now, in this moment, in this life.

Ascension — Seated with Christ in heavenly places — not one day, not only in theory — now. That is our current, actual position.

Awakening: Restorative Metanoia — The true awakening begins to fully unfold. The original Greek opens up and the beauty of the gospel — hidden in plain sight for centuries — comes alive in ways religion never reached.

The Awakening Glossary: Companion Resource — The language of awakening — distilled, portable, and designed to accelerate everything the series unlocks.

Heavenly Health Hacks: God's Design for Vibrant Living — Coming Soon — Another revelation track: God's original design for spirit, soul, and body. Health isn't separate from the gospel — it's an expression of it.

Living Awakened: Coming Soon — Walking it out daily. What does life look like fully lived from the finished work?

Each revelation built on the last. None of it was planned — it was led. And that's the point: awakening isn't achieved. It isn't even received in the sense of doing something to get it. It's a place of rest. A place of being. Of simply knowing. It rises from within — the same way the Kingdom does.

The Fruit of Awakening

And what surfaces as the fog lifts is not new — it was always there. Joy is not something that departed and now comes back — it is the atmosphere of union with Christ, which is inseparable and permanent. What awakening restores is your awareness of the joy that was always present, obscured by sin-consciousness and the performance exhaustion of religion. The same is true of rest — not a reward waiting at the end of better obedience, but your natural state as someone held in blameless innocence in Him. And hope shifts — not from absence to presence, but from fragile and future-tense to certain and now, anchored in a finished work. These aren't destinations you arrive at. They are what becomes visible when the striving stops and union becomes your awareness. And then something else becomes visible: you stop looking inward and start seeing others.

"To discover your own completeness in Christ frees you to turn your attention away from yourself to others. The way Jesus saw himself is the only valid way to see yourself."
— Philippians 2:4–5 (MSB)

This is agape — the natural overflow of union. When you know who you are, you are finally free to tell others who they are. Not who they were in themselves. Who they have always been in Christ. Awakening was never meant to end with you.

Something worth naming: going deeper into these things doesn't always feel like clarity at first. There is a learning and an unlearning happening simultaneously. Old frameworks resist. Familiar verses look different. What once settled now opens. That disorientation isn't doubt — it's the fog lifting. It's what metanoia actually feels like from the inside. Confusion in the process isn't a sign you're going wrong. It's often a sign you're going deeper.

This journey unfolded one step at a time for one person. That same journey is available to everyone.

What the Language Reveals

The words were hiding in plain sight the whole time.

I approach everything the way an engineer would — layer by layer: if this is true, what does that mean? And if that's true, what changes? Applied to the original Greek of the New Testament, that

process cracked everything wide open.

These aren't complicated discoveries. They're small. Precise. And each one changes how you read every page of Scripture.

Or this: the word translated "all" — pas — means all. Every. Without exception. No conditions. No fine print. When God says all, He means all.

Take one example: the word "if" in Paul's letters. When Paul writes "if you are in Christ" — the Greek isn't a condition. It's a conclusion. A better translation is "since." Since you are in Christ. Since this is already true. The cage door was never locked. You just didn't know it.

Or this: the word we translate as "truth" — aletheia — doesn't mean a correct proposition to defend. It means unveiled reality. Truth isn't an argument. It's a veil being lifted. And when you hold that alongside awakening — restored perception, sight returning — you realize they're describing the same movement from two directions. Awakening is what it feels like when aletheia arrives.

Or this: the word translated "perish" or "lost" — apollumi — isn't destruction or eternal torment. It's the lost coin. The lost son. Missing your God-given purpose, wandering from your true identity. Consider John 3:16 — perhaps the most quoted verse in all of Christianity. "Whoever believes in him shall not perish." When you understand what perish actually means — not annihilation, but living lost from your purpose, cut off from who you were designed to be — the verse opens into something infinitely more personal. God didn't send His Son so you could escape destruction. He sent His Son so you could come home to yourself.

Or this: the word we translate as "faith" — pistis — isn't something you generate. It originates in God. You're not summoning belief hard enough; you're receiving what God already believes about you. His faithfulness, flowing through you.

Or this: "new creation" doesn't mean something brand new that never existed. It means true creation — the original design, finally restored. What was always intended, now unveiled.

Or this: awakening — metanoia — isn't guilt or turning from sin. It's restored perception. Your sight coming back. Seeing what was always there, hidden behind the fog of religion.

We don't live toward the finished work. We live from it. Tetelestai — "it is finished" — is in the Greek perfect tense: completed action with permanent results. That's our starting line, not our finish line.

And perhaps the most stunning: you were never a surprise to God. You have never been known differently than you are known right now. You were chosen before the foundation of the world — and awakening is simply the moment you begin to remember it.

Here is what all of it points to: Jesus is All in All. Not mostly. Not primarily. All. Our union with Him is inseparable — and we contributed nothing to it. We stand before God blameless and

innocent, not because of anything we brought, but because of everything He is. It is entirely by grace, so that no man can boast. The awakening isn't adding something to what He did. It's realizing He already did it all — and that includes you.

And this: God only thinks good of you. Not mostly good. Not good when you perform well. Only good. Always. That's not a motivational thought — it's the logical conclusion of grace. If the finished work is complete and union is inseparable, then there is no version of you that God views with anything other than delight.

Or this: the early Church Fathers had a word for what union with Christ actually produces — theosis. Participation in the divine nature. Not becoming God in essence, but becoming by grace what He is by nature. Here's what most Western Christianity doesn't know: the early Church didn't frame salvation primarily as a legal transaction — that framework came centuries later, through Latin theology and Western courts. For the first thousand years of Christianity, the primary understanding of salvation was theosis. Union. Restoration of image. Athanasius said it plainly: "God became man so that man might become god." Not God in essence — but participants in His divine life. As Peter writes: "His divine engineering gifted us with all that it takes to live life to the full... our restored participation in our godly origin" (2 Peter 1:3-4, MSB). Religion offered forgiveness and distance. The gospel — the original gospel — restores you to your original design. Fully human, radiant with divine life. Think of a candle placed in fire: it remains a candle, but takes on the properties of the flame.

Here's the frame that holds all of it together: your spirit already knows these things. It has always known. Awakening is the soul catching up to what the spirit already carries as true — waking from the illusion of separation into the reality of a union that was always there. Consciousness is the arena where that catching-up happens — where what is eternally settled in your spirit begins to surface in how you think, see, and live.

Which means the real enemy was never God's wrath. It was never your failures. The real enemy is sin-consciousness — the fog of identity amnesia that keeps the soul asleep to what the spirit already knows. Hamartia isn't moral crime. It's forgetting who you are. And the antidote isn't trying harder — it's awakening to righteousness-consciousness. Knowing at the level of your soul what God has always known about you.

Once you see it, you cannot unsee it.

Welcome Home

You were never outside God's love—only blind to your eternal inclusion in His embrace. The love that flows eternally between Father, Son, and Spirit—this triune love—is the catalyst for all awakening. It dreamed you, designed you, and now draws you home to what you have always been.

You haven't been taught who to become. You've been reintroduced to who you've always been.

The Greek words weren't information to acquire—they were mirrors helping you remember what you forgot.

Awakening isn't learning. It's remembering.

Tetelestai — It is finished. Remember. *En Christō* — You are in Him. Remember. *Metanoia* — Now you see. Remember.

"In him, all the fullness of Deity resides in a human body. He proves that human life is tailor-made for God. We are complete in him. Jesus mirrors our wholeness and endorses our true identity. He is I AM in us." — Colossians 2:9–10 (MSB)

Read that again: COMPLETE. Not "becoming complete." Not "will be complete if we fight hard enough." Complete. Now. Already.

To know Jesus is to know yourself — identity restored.

You were created by love and for love. You were found in Christ before you were lost in Adam. You were loved before you were born. You were home before you wandered. You have always been His.

You're not just saved. You're not just forgiven. You're not just accepted.

You're HOME.

There is no place like home—in Him. There is no place like heaven—within. God is home in you — and we are His address. Seamless union.

Heaven is where God is — and you are where God is. Heaven is a person. Jesus!

This is your awakening. This is your remembering. Welcome home.

What This Resource Contains

This companion piece distills two essential elements from the full book into a portable reference you can return to again and again:

The Essential Awakening Glossary unlocks the original Greek meanings behind the words we read in Scripture. For centuries, translation choices have obscured the radical beauty of the gospel. When you understand what words like *metanoia, tetelestai,* and *hamartia* actually mean, familiar verses come alive with fresh revelation. This is not merely a dictionary—it is a transformation tool that shifts your understanding from reward-language to gift-language.

The Key Awakening Scriptures form the biblical foundation of awakening theology. The full book contains over 1,000 scripture references—but we have distilled the key verses that capture the essence of the awakening message. Each has been carefully selected to reinforce your true identity in Christ. They are perfect for morning declarations, moments of doubt, or whenever you need an immediate reminder of who you really are.

How to Use This Resource

This is not meant to be read once and set aside. It's a daily companion — something you pick up in the morning to declare truth, or reach for when the old vocabulary tries to pull you back.

For first-time readers: begin with Section 1 — The Most Essential Terms. Master Tetelestai, Metanoia, and En Christō first. These three unlock everything else in the glossary.

For daily practice: choose one Greek term per week. Read the full entry slowly. Speak the declaration aloud. Let the truth settle before moving to the next. There is no rush — awakening is not a destination to reach but a reality to inhabit.

When you feel stuck — when performance thinking creeps back, or identity confusion sets in, or condemnation whispers — turn to the How to Use This Glossary guide on page 21. It maps exactly which terms speak to what you're facing, and walks you through a simple reset process to return to truth.

And when you're ready to go deeper, the full journey awaits.

You're not learning something new.
You're waking up to what was always there.
Welcome home.

The Invitation

Remember: you are not learning new truths here. You are awakening to truths that have always been. You are not earning what you do not have—you are receiving what has already been given. You are not becoming something new—you are recognizing who you have always been. God believes in you!

"Tetelestai. It is finished. Now live from it."

We Believe:

- The Bible is God's inspired Word and our authoritative guide for life
- We affirm the Apostles' Creed and the Nicene Creed (325 AD)—established by the early Church Fathers as the foundational truths of the Christian faith—and the Trinity: one God in three persons—Father, Son, and Holy Spirit—co-equal and co-eternal
- Jesus Christ is fully God and fully man, born of the Virgin Mary, crucified under Pontius Pilate, risen bodily on the third day, ascended to the Father, and coming again in glory. He is the only way to the Father, not one option among many
- It is the goodness of God that opens our eyes (Romans 2:4). When we see Jesus for who He truly is, we begin to see ourselves for who we truly are—and awakening begins. Salvation is a gift already given; receiving and acknowledging Jesus as Lord, believing God raised Him from the dead (Romans 10:9 NIV NIV)—this is our "yes" that begins the awakening process. The gift must be received
- Salvation is by grace alone—not earned, not deserved, not achieved (Ephesians 2:8-9 NIV). Grace is not merely forgiveness; it is God's divine empowerment, transforming us from the inside out (Titus 2:11-12 NIV)
- Transformation flows from identity, not behavior. Holiness and righteousness are the natural fruit of knowing who we are in Christ—we don't journey toward holiness, we live from it
- Sin is serious—it destroys life, wastes purpose, and produces real suffering. Awakening theology takes sin more seriously, not less, because we understand what it costs
- God's justice is restorative, not retributive—He corrects to restore, not punishes to destroy. What Scripture calls "wrath" is God's faithfulness to truth, the principle of sowing and reaping built into reality itself
- God's design for human flourishing, revealed in Scripture, is perfect

A Note on Our Foundation

We intentionally anchor our faith in the Apostles' Creed and Nicene Creed—the earliest consensus statements of the Christian Church, written by leaders who still read the New Testament in its original Greek. These creeds declare who God is and what He has done: Father, Son, and Holy Spirit; the incarnation, crucifixion, resurrection, and return of Jesus Christ.

What's remarkable is what these creeds *don't* say. They don't prescribe penal substitutionary atonement. They don't define eternal conscious torment. They don't mention total depravity, original sin, or a mechanical formula for salvation. Those frameworks were added centuries later—largely through Latin translations and Western theological traditions that the early Church Fathers never endorsed.

Liberal theology waters down the Gospel into human philosophy. The awakening message does the opposite—it amplifies the Gospel by returning to what the original Greek text actually says and what the early Church Fathers understood about Christ's complete victory and our union with Him. This isn't a departure from historic Christianity. It's a return to it—recovering the original Greek meanings that the earliest believers understood and the creeds preserved. We aren't adding to the faith. We're uncovering what was always there.

Two Gospels:
The Shift That Changes Everything

For centuries, two very different gospels have been preached—often from the same pulpit, using the same Bible. One speaks the language of separation and condition. The other speaks the language of union and completion.

The difference isn't simply theological preference. It's the difference between:

- **Striving** and **resting**
- **Earning (reward)** and **receiving (gift)**
- **Orphan-thinking** and **son-thinking**
- **The gospel of "do"** and **the gospel of "done"**

The beautiful gospel is the announcement of seamless union—that we are already in Christ.

Traditional Gospel Understanding

The gospel of "do" — Salvation begins a process of becoming; we must do our part to maintain, grow, and prove our salvation

All have sinned and fall short of the glory of God — Sin creates separation between us and God

We are born sinners — Our fundamental identity is that of sinners in need of rescue

God hates sin — Sin is moral failure and rebellion against God; breaking His laws; God's holiness cannot tolerate sin and it must be punished

Awakening Gospel Understanding

The gospel of "done" — *Tetelestai*—it is finished; we awaken to a completed work, not complete one ourselves

All have missed the mark (hamartia) of their true identity — We've lived blind to who we are; sin doesn't separate us from God's love—it blinds us to the glory we already possess

We were found in Christ before we were lost in Adam — Our origin is divine; our true identity is beloved sons and daughters.

Sin (hamartia) is 'missing the mark' of your true identity — Sin is identity amnesia; it blinds us to who we are but doesn't change who we are in God's eyes. The bad decisions and destructive behaviors that flow from that amnesia produce real consequences — not punishment from an angry God, but the natural harvest of living outside our design. Wrath is never punitive; it is always restorative.

Traditional Gospel Understanding	Awakening Gospel Understanding
Sin requires punishment — Crime against a holy God demanding justice and wrath	**Sin is disease requiring healing** — Sickness needing cure, not crime needing punishment; wrath is sin's natural consequence, not God's imposed penalty
Faith is our response to God — We must believe in order to be saved; faith originates in our decision	**Faith flows from God to us** — From faith (source) to faith (recipient); God's faith is the basis of our belief; *here, faith happens!*
New creation begins at conversion — You become a new creation the moment you profess faith; before that, you were the old creation	**New Creation, Kainos** = Already new in nature/quality — *Kainos* means new in essence, not time; the new creation reality was established at the cross and exists whether you've awakened to it or not; faith reveals what's already true, it doesn't create it (2 Cor 5:17)
Being "born again" happens after a decision — Salvation begins when we accept Christ; we receive the Kingdom and the Holy Spirit enters us at conversion	**Being "born from above" (anōthen) is awakening to the Kingdom already within** — Jesus declared "The Kingdom of God is within you" (Luke 17:21 NIV) before the cross; "We did not begin in our mother's womb! We began in God!" (MSB); this awakening begins when we receive and acknowledge Jesus
The Spirit enters at conversion — The Holy Spirit comes into us when we believe; we receive the Spirit as a result of our decision	**The Spirit reveals union** — The Spirit doesn't create union—He reveals the union that always existed; He flows FROM within, not TO you from outside; at Pentecost, the Spirit didn't arrive—He became evident
Jesus became sin — He took on our sinfulness so we could become righteous	**Jesus entered our hell, our darkness** — He didn't satisfy a wrathful Father; He revealed a loving one who came to find us; the Word became *sarx*—entering fully into our flesh, our junk, our brokenness—to heal us from within

Traditional Gospel Understanding	Awakening Gospel Understanding
God is a God of justice and holy wrath — Sin must be punished; a holy God cannot tolerate sin; His wrath demands satisfaction	**God's justice is restorative, not punitive —** His "wrath" is not a temper tantrum but His faithfulness to truth—the principle of sowing and reaping built into reality itself. Love burns away everything that blinds us to truth; justice heals and makes right, not destroys
Jesus died to satisfy God's wrath — The cross was payment to appease divine justice (penal substitution)	**Jesus entered into our condition to bring us home —** The cross wasn't payment demanded by God; it was rescue initiated by God
Redemption is rescue from damnation — Jesus paid the price to buy us back from Satan or God's wrath	**Redeemed means recovering what was yours** — You can only redeem what already belonged to you; God didn't purchase you from a stranger—He recovered what was always His
Reconciliation is making peace with an angry God — We were enemies who needed to appease God's wrath through Christ's sacrifice	**Reconciled means prior connection restored** — You can only reconcile with someone you were first connected to; "God was reconciling the world to Himself in Christ, not counting people's sins against them" (2 Cor 5:19 NIV)—not punishment, not wrath, not counting
Restoration is future hope — All things will be made new someday in heaven; we wait for future glory	**Restored means returning to original design** — You can only restore what originally existed; there was an original design—Eden restored, not escaped; you're returning to who you always were
Hell is eternal conscious torment — A place of permanent punishment where God sends the unrepentant; eternal separation from God with no possibility of restoration	**Hell (Gehenna) is restorative, not eternal —** The Greek *aiōnios* means "age-during," not everlasting; God's fire purifies rather than punishes; as Isaac of Nineveh wrote, those in Gehenna are "scourged by the scourge of love"—leading ultimately to restoration

Traditional Gospel Understanding	Awakening Gospel Understanding
Adoption into God's family — We were orphans who become children through faith; outsiders brought in	**Adoption (huiothesia) means "coming of age"** — We were always sons and daughters; *huiothesia* was the Roman ceremony where an existing child was declared mature heir with full rights—we awaken to inheritance, not become children we weren't
Performance-based living — Our standing with God depends on our obedience, effort, and spiritual disciplines	**Position-based living** — Your standing was established by Christ's performance, not yours; you're already seated in heavenly places (Ephesians 2:6 NIV); a servant works to earn a place at the table, but a son simply sits down because he belongs
Striving for holiness — We work to become sanctified and holy through discipline and spiritual effort	**Expressing holiness** — You ARE holy in Christ (1 Peter 2:9 NIV)—set apart, included in the Trinity's communion. The journey isn't toward holiness but FROM holiness—not achieving sanctification but expressing the sanctification you already possess. Holiness is awakening to—and remembering—who you already are, because behavior flows from identity
Waiting for revival — We pray for God to come down and move among us; revival is a future event we hope and long for	**Revival is within** — The Kingdom of God is within you (Luke 17:21 NIV); Christ in you is the hope of glory; you're not waiting for God to show up—you're awakening to the God who never left
Free will requires a decision — We must make Jesus Lord in order to be saved	**God acted while we were blinded** — He entered our darkness before we were in our right minds; free will begins the awakening process, not salvation itself

Traditional Gospel Understanding

Confession brings us across the bridge — Our declaration of faith moves us from separation to salvation

Jesus is THE way, the truth, and the life — No one comes to the Father except through Him; He is the only path to salvation; our choice to accept Him determines our eternal destiny

Salvation is a gift we receive when we believe — The gift is offered; we must accept it

"It is finished"—but our work continues — The cross is complete, but Jesus did His part, now we must do ours; salvation is available to those who accept it

Awakening Gospel Understanding

Reconciliation was accomplished before we believed — Faith doesn't create our salvation; it opens our eyes to see the salvation already accomplished; confession is the "yes" that begins the awakening as our response to the Father's love

Jesus is THE way, the ultimate truth, the ultimate reality — He is the singular door through which all must enter; our free will is the awakening response—we must choose to enter through the door, to step into the light of what's already true; Jesus is not one option among many, He is THE reality, and our part is to awaken and walk through

Salvation is a total grace gift — Already given before we believed, based on the faithfulness of God; yet a gift must be received. As people hear the beautiful gospel, the power of the gospel awakens them to respond to the Father's love

Tetelestai — Finished and remains forever finished (perfect tense); nothing left to add, earn, or complete; the place of rest; God was reconciling the world to Himself in Christ (2 Cor 5:19 NIV); awakening begins when we receive Jesus and acknowledge what is already true

A Deeper Foundation

The shift in this table is not theological preference. It is a recovery of the original gospel — and it begins before creation.

Union is the foundational reality. Not sin. Not separation. Union. Before the first breath, before the fall, before time itself — you were chosen in Christ (Ephesians 1:4 NIV) and the Lamb was already slain (Revelation 13:8 NIV). The union was never broken. The inseparable oneness of Creator and creation — of Father and beloved — is the bedrock on which everything else rests. Nothing that happened in time changed what was established in eternity.

Which means sin entered a story where its defeat was already written. It was a dethroned monarch — stripped of its throne before it ever claimed one. Its record removed as far as the east is from the west (Psalm 103:12 NIV). Its power broken at a cross that existed in God's eternal intention before the world was made. You stand before God not as a sinner being tolerated but as one declared blameless and innocent in Him — not because sin is dismissed, but because it was defeated before it began.

Separation, then, was never the real story. It was the illusion — the experience of distance that arose from identity amnesia, not from any change in God's posture toward us. The union never broke. Only our awareness of it did. And what religion framed as moral failure and behavioral crime was always, at its root, a blindness problem. A perception problem. A forgetting problem. Sin is the consequence of living outside your true identity — the destructive fruit of amnesia — not a crime that defines you or a wall that divides you from God.

The early church knew this. For a thousand years, the gospel was theosis — union with God, participation in divine life, the restoration of image. Athanasius said it plainly: "God became man so that man might become god" — not God in essence, but partakers of His divine nature (2 Peter 1:4). Not: fix your behavior and earn your standing. But: wake up to the union that was always there. The performance-religion machine came later — built not on Scripture but on a single translation choice. Jerome rendered metanoia as paenitentia. Perception-shift became penance. A healing gospel became an earning gospel. A blindness problem became a crime problem. The confusion around sin that fills the church today is not a failure of devotion. It is the fruit of an inherited frame.

Awakening theology is not a departure from historic Christianity. It is a return to it. To the gospel the early church preached, the gospel encoded in the Greek, the gospel the Lamb sealed in eternity before time began.

The Language Itself Reveals the Truth

The very vocabulary of the gospel proves you belonged before you were lost:

Redeemed — You can only redeem what already belonged to you. **Reconciled** — You can only reconcile with someone you were first connected to. **Restored** — You can only restore what originally existed.

Innocence — restored! Likeness — redeemed! Friendship — reconciled!

But how? Through the most stunning act in history: **the Incarnation.**

When the Word became *sarx*, God didn't reach down from a distance to rescue you — He entered fully into your humanity. All your weakness. All your brokenness. All your flesh. He didn't heal you from the outside; He healed you from within. The Divine fused with the human so that humanity could be restored to its original design.

This is why even the word **sin** (*hamartia*) means "missing the mark" — not crime requiring punishment, but blindness requiring healing. You were never a criminal needing a judge. You were a beloved child needing to be awakened to who you always were.

Welcome to your new vocabulary. Welcome to your new reality. Welcome home.

When My Spirit Leaps

When I first opened the Mirror Study Bible, my spirit leaped. There was a deep resonance—truth being unveiled, not learned. Something in me said, *"Yes. This is what I've always known but couldn't articulate."*

And it hasn't stopped. Every time I open it, my spirit leaps again. The truth doesn't grow stale. Each encounter takes me deeper, and my spirit keeps recognizing home.

The fruit I've witnessed from those who receive the beautiful gospel:

Freedom—religious performance chains broken. **Joy**—the settled gladness of a son who knows he belongs. **Peace**—the profound rest of one who knows the work is finished. **Rest**—the confident exhale of someone no longer striving to earn what was always freely given.

Religion demanded more. The beautiful gospel declares, *"It is finished."*

And in that declaration, my spirit finally came home.

A Note on Greek Sources

All Greek word studies are cross-referenced with reputable lexical sources for scholarly integrity.

An Important Note on Strong's Concordance: Throughout this glossary, you'll see Strong's numbers included for accessibility. However, Strong's (1890) was never designed as a lexicon—James Strong himself called his definitions "brief and simple" glosses. Since then, two developments have transformed Greek scholarship:

1. **The Papyri Discoveries (early 1900s):** Thousands of Greek texts revealed that New Testament Greek was Koine (common) Greek—the everyday language of first-century people

2. **Modern Lexical Scholarship:** The academic standard is now BDAG (Bauer-Danker-Arndt-Gingrich), incorporating over a century of additional research.

Primary Sources for This Glossary:

- **BDAG** — The most authoritative modern Greek-English lexicon of the New Testament
- **Louw-Nida** — Greek-English Lexicon based on semantic domains
- **LSJ** (Liddell-Scott-Jones) — Comprehensive Greek-English lexicon
- **The Mirror Study Bible** — Francois du Toit's extensive Greek analysis
- **Strong's Concordance** — Included for numerical cross-referencing

About Interpretations: Some interpretations represent minority scholarly positions (particularly *aionios*, *huiothesia, apokatastasis*), while others reflect well-established patristic theology (*theosis, perichoresis*). All are lexically and biblically defensible. Our goal: scholarly integrity and spiritual awakening—showing you not just what these words mean, but what they mean *for you.*

About The Mirror Study Bible

Throughout this glossary—and this entire book—you'll encounter extensive references to *The Mirror Study Bible* (MSB) by Francois du Toit. This deserves explanation, because for many readers, the MSB translations will seem radically different from what they've known.

What the Mirror Study Bible Is

The Mirror Study Bible is a paraphrased translation—similar in approach to the Amplified Bible, The Message, and The Passion Translation. It is not a word-for-word literal translation but an expanded text designed to reveal the fuller meaning embedded in the original Greek.

In Francois du Toit's own words:

> *The Mirror Study Bible is a paraphrased translation from the Greek text. While strictly following the literal meaning of the original, sentences have been constructed so that the larger meaning is continually emphasized by means of an expanded text.*

> *Some clarifying notes are included in italics. This is a paraphrased study rather than a literal translation. While the detailed shades of meaning of every Greek word and its components have been closely studied, this is done taking into account the consistent context of the entire chapter within the wider epistle, and bearing in mind that Jesus is what the Scriptures are all about and humankind is what Jesus is all about.*

> *To assist the reader in their study, I have numerically superscripted the Greek word and corresponded it with the closest English word in the italicized commentary that follows. This is to create a direct comparison of words between the two languages.*

This approach—expanded text that unpacks the full meaning of Greek words while maintaining consistent context—is what makes the MSB such a powerful awakening tool.

The Scholar Behind the Work

Francois du Toit brings rigorous academic training to his translation work. He studied Greek and

Hebrew for three years at the University of Pretoria (1975-1977) and regularly consults established scholarly resources including:

- *The Textual Commentary of The Greek New Testament* by Bruce Metzger
- *Analytical Greek Lexicon* by Wesley J. Perschbacher

What distinguishes du Toit's approach is his deep commitment to etymology—carefully considering the individual values of the various components within each Greek word. As he explains:

> "I constantly consider the individual values of the various components in each Greek word—thus arriving at deeper meanings of the word that is not always reflected in other Lexicons."

This etymological approach is why MSB definitions often feel more expansive than traditional translations. Du Toit isn't adding to Scripture—he's unpacking what was always embedded in the original Greek but compressed or obscured through centuries of translation choices.

Academic Recognition

On June 11, 2022, Francois du Toit was awarded a PhD in theology and philosophy based on his Mirror Study Bible work. Dr. Douglas J. Wingate, President and Founder of Life Christian University, offered this assessment:

> *"We consider it a great honor to be the academic institution that first had the opportunity to recognize your incredible work producing the Mirror Study Bible. The spiritual insight that you reveal along with your thorough exegesis amazes me. I have had many favorite translations over the years, but none that elevates me to experience such glorious heavenly communion as the Mirror. The world will be forever indebted to you for such a powerful gift of The Mirror Word, and a true understanding of God's Kingdom and His overwhelming love for His creation and family."*

Why This Matters for Your Awakening

The MSB isn't trying to replace other translations—it's trying to recover what other translations couldn't fully convey. Where traditional versions often compress rich Greek concepts into single English words, the MSB expands them to reveal their full scope.

This is why familiar verses suddenly come alive when you encounter them in the MSB. You're not reading a different Bible—you're seeing depths in the same Bible that were always there but hidden beneath centuries of theological and linguistic assumptions.

As you journey through this glossary, let the MSB translations challenge you. Where they seem unfamiliar, remember: these aren't novel interpretations. They're ancient meanings that older tools couldn't fully capture. The awakening message isn't new—it's been there in the Greek all along.

How to Use This Glossary

This isn't a dictionary to skim—it's a transformation tool.

For First-Time Readers:

- Read "The Most Essential Terms" (Section 1) before starting Chapter 1
- Master **Tetelestai, Metanoia,** and **En Christō** first—these three unlock everything
- Return to the glossary as you encounter terms throughout the book

For Daily Practice:

- Choose one Greek term per week
- Read the entire entry *slowly*, multiple times
- Meditate on its "Awakening Impact"
- Speak the "In Practice" declaration aloud
- Journal how living from this truth changes your day

When You Feel Stuck:

If struggling with...   Go to...

Performance mindset   Tetelestai, Dikaiosune, Charis

Identity confusion   Hamartia, Morphē, En Christō

Striving and trying harder   Pistis, Charis, Teleios

Fear of judgment   Krino, Katallassō, Kolasis

Feeling separated from God   En Christō, Perichoresis, Union Reality

Condemnation and guilt   Hamartia, Metanoia, Apollumi

The Reset Process:

1. Identify which lie you're believing (old vocabulary)

2. Find the corresponding Greek truth (new vocabulary)

3. Speak the "In Practice" declaration over yourself

4. Journal the shift in consciousness you experience

Understanding the Two Diagrams

The One Truth That Changes Everything

Before we look at these diagrams, we need to establish the one reality Paul couldn't stop repeating. Over 160 times in his letters, he returns to the same phrase: *in Christ.*

Not "toward Christ." Not "working for Christ." Not "hoping to reach Christ." In Him. Already. Now.

This is your location before it is your experience. This is your address before it is your awareness. Whatever you believe about yourself, whatever you feel on any given day — the settled, unchangeable, resurrection-established truth is this: you are in Christ.

Everything in these two diagrams flows from that single reality. These two diagrams work together to reveal both the reality of your union with God and the journey of awakening to it.

The Four Circles shows what is eternally true — the seamless union that has always existed. Jesus declared: "I am in my Father, and you are in me, and I am in you" (John 14:20 NIV). This single verse contains the entire reality — the Father contains all, Jesus is in the Father, you are in Jesus, the Spirit is in you. There is no gap, no distance, no separation. Heaven is not a place you go — it is a reality you recognize. You are already there. You just haven't fully seen it yet.

The Awakening Journey shows how we come to see what has always been true. At the cross, Jesus declared "Tetelestai" — It is finished (John 19:30). The Greek perfect tense means completed action with permanent results. Everything in these diagrams flows from that finished work.

You were found in Christ before you were lost in Adam (Ephesians 1:4 NIV). The fall was not a change in God's design but a change in our perception. We became trapped in unbelief — the Greek apeitheia means "un-persuadedness," not rebellion. We lived below our design, blind to our true identity.

Then God's kindness breaks through. Romans 2:4 (NIV) declares it is His kindness and love — not guilt, not fear, not threat of punishment — that leads us to metanoia. This is the engine of transformation: not our effort to change, but His relentless goodness that opens our eyes. The Greek word metanoia (meta = beyond + nous = mind/perception) does not mean guilt-driven repentance. Jerome's Latin translation corrupted it into "penance." The original means transformation of perception — seeing what you couldn't see before.

This is where we receive Jesus. Our hearts open to the revelation that He is the Son of God. We say "yes" to what He has already said "yes" to us. As John declares: "To all who received him, he gave the right to become children of God" (John 1:12 NIV). Not becoming something we weren't — receiving authority to live as who we always were.

"Everyone who realizes their association in him, convinced that he is their original life and that his name defines them, God gives the assurance that they are indeed his offspring, begotten of him; he sanctions the legitimacy of their sonship." (John 1:12 MSB)

Make no mistake — a gift unacknowledged remains unopened. This is not universalism; it is invitation awaiting response. The reality is complete; our "yes" opens our eyes to it.

From here, the mind is renewed. We move from sin-consciousness to righteousness-consciousness. From orphan-thinking to son-thinking. From striving to resting. This is Christ-consciousness — the progressive revelation of our identity and righteousness already secured in Him.

The Power Source: What Moves You Through the Triangle

The triangle might look like a mountain you climb. It isn't.

Paul makes an astonishing claim: the identical energy (energeia) that raised Christ's dead body from the tomb is the power currently working (energeō) in you — energizing both your desire to awaken AND your capacity to respond.

"For it is God who works in you to will and to act in order to fulfill his good purpose."
(Philippians 2:13 NIV)

Same word family. Same power Paul describes in Ephesians 1:19-20 — the working (energeia) of God's mighty strength that raised Christ from the dead.

You don't ascend the triangle through effort — resurrection power carries you. The movement from "The Faith That Saves" toward "The Allness of God" isn't powered by discipline. It's powered by the same force that reversed death. This power isn't impersonal — it is the Spirit of Truth Himself, the same Spirit who raised Christ, now living in you (Romans 8:11), awakening you to what has always been true (John 16:13).

Your role? Yield and enter rest. You already have the mind of Christ in your heart (1 Corinthians 2:16). Rest celebrates the finished work, abandons every effort to improve what God has perfected, and allows the Spirit to become the ruling influence. This is the position of grace.

This is gift language, not reward language. You don't earn your way into the circles. You don't scale the triangle through performance. You receive what was always given and awaken to what was always true — carried by the same resurrection energy that raised Christ.

This is the already/awakening tension: everything is already complete in heaven's reality, yet we progressively awaken to it in earthly experience. The work is finished; the seeing unfolds. And the power that accomplishes both? Not yours. His.

The Four Circles answers: What is true? **The Awakening Journey** answers: How do I awaken to what is true? **Energeō** answers: What power makes it happen?

Seamless Union — *The Four Circles*

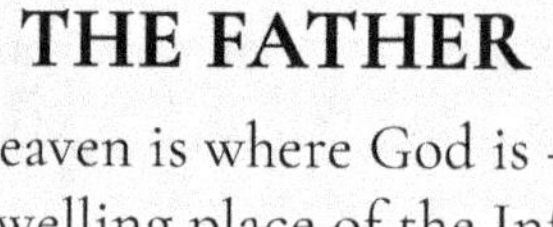

THE FATHER

Heaven is where God is —
the dwelling place of the Infinite
The encompassing reality

JESUS

"I am in My Father" —
Jesus is in the Father

John 10:30

YOU

"You are in Me" —
En Christo, your location

John 14:20

HOLY SPIRIT

"I am in you" —
The Spirit indwells you

John 14:20

The Key Insight

John 14:20 — *"I am in My Father, and you are in Me, and I am in you."*

This is the nesting:
- Father contains all
- Jesus is IN the Father
- You are IN Jesus
- Spirit is IN you

There is no gap. No distance. No separation.
You are encapsulated in love — all the way down.

The Theological Point: *Heaven is within*

Luke 17:21 — *"For indeed, the kingdom of God is within you."*

Heaven is not a place you go. Heaven is where God is.

If God is the Father... And Jesus is in the Father... And you are in Jesus... And the Spirit is in you...

Then you are already in heaven. You just haven't fully awakened to it.

Colossians 3:3 — *"Your life is hidden with Christ in God."*

Hidden. Nested. Encapsulated. Safe. Home.

You are from heaven! You are where heaven and earth meet.

The Awakening Journey

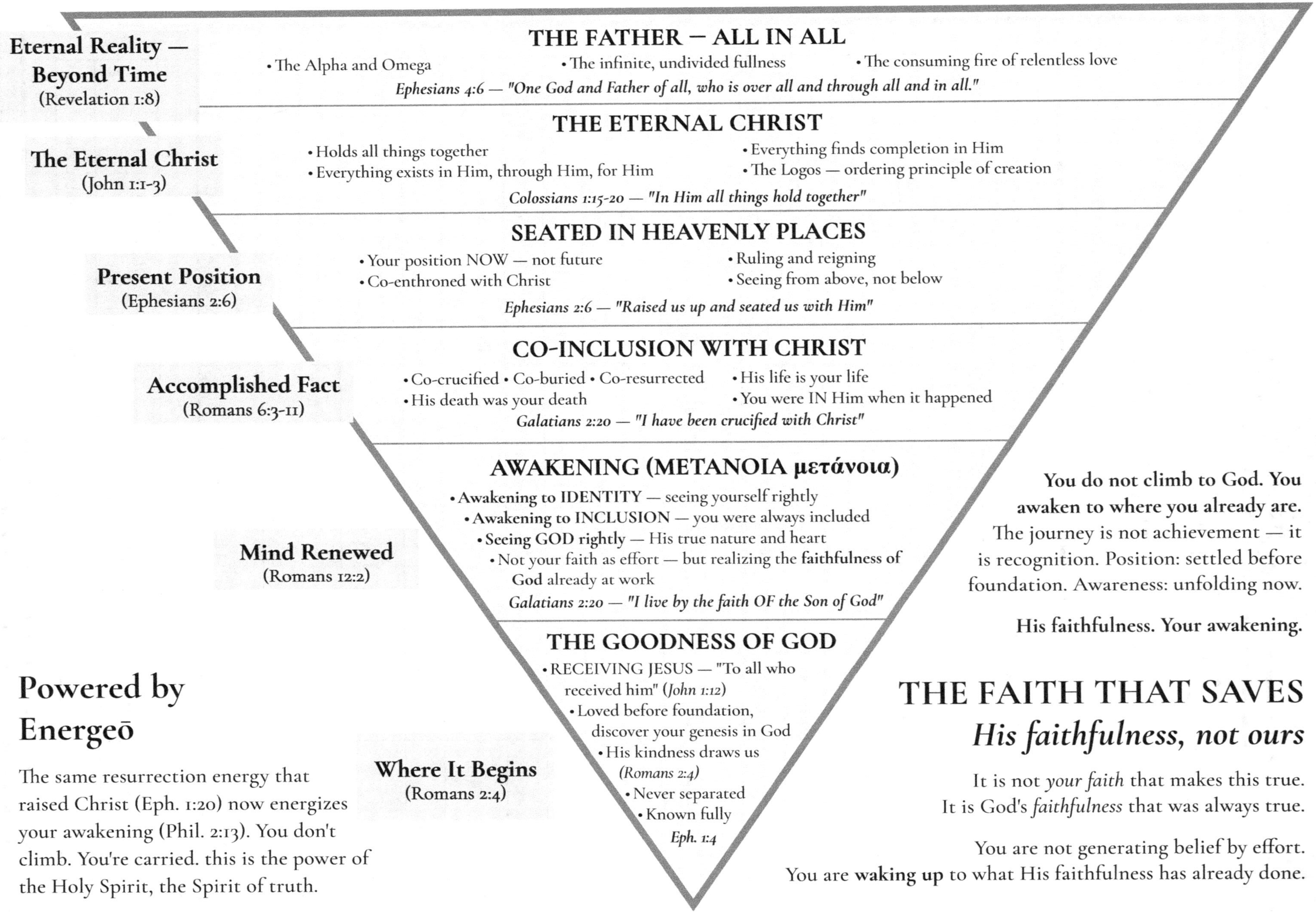

Eternal Reality — Beyond Time
(Revelation 1:8)

THE FATHER — ALL IN ALL

- The Alpha and Omega
- The infinite, undivided fullness
- The consuming fire of relentless love

Ephesians 4:6 — "One God and Father of all, who is over all and through all and in all."

The Eternal Christ
(John 1:1-3)

THE ETERNAL CHRIST

- Holds all things together
- Everything exists in Him, through Him, for Him
- Everything finds completion in Him
- The Logos — ordering principle of creation

Colossians 1:15-20 — "In Him all things hold together"

Present Position
(Ephesians 2:6)

SEATED IN HEAVENLY PLACES

- Your position NOW — not future
- Co-enthroned with Christ
- Ruling and reigning
- Seeing from above, not below

Ephesians 2:6 — "Raised us up and seated us with Him"

Accomplished Fact
(Romans 6:3-11)

CO-INCLUSION WITH CHRIST

- Co-crucified • Co-buried • Co-resurrected
- His death was your death
- His life is your life
- You were IN Him when it happened

Galatians 2:20 — "I have been crucified with Christ"

Mind Renewed
(Romans 12:2)

AWAKENING (METANOIA μετάνοια)

- Awakening to IDENTITY — seeing yourself rightly
- Awakening to INCLUSION — you were always included
- Seeing GOD rightly — His true nature and heart
- Not your faith as effort — but realizing the **faithfulness of God** already at work

Galatians 2:20 — "I live by the faith OF the Son of God"

THE GOODNESS OF GOD

- RECEIVING JESUS — "To all who received him" (*John 1:12*)
- Loved before foundation, discover your genesis in God
- His kindness draws us (*Romans 2:4*)
- Never separated
- Known fully

Eph. 1:4

Where It Begins
(Romans 2:4)

You do not climb to God. You awaken to where you already are.
The journey is not achievement — it is recognition. Position: settled before foundation. Awareness: unfolding now.

His faithfulness. Your awakening.

THE FAITH THAT SAVES
His faithfulness, not ours

It is not *your faith* that makes this true.
It is God's *faithfulness* that was always true.

You are not generating belief by effort.
You are **waking up** to what His faithfulness has already done.

Powered by Energeō

The same resurrection energy that raised Christ (Eph. 1:20) now energizes your awakening (Phil. 2:13). You don't climb. You're carried. this is the power of the Holy Spirit, the Spirit of truth.

Quick Reference Index with Pronunciation Guide

Use this table to quickly locate terms and learn how to speak them aloud.

Section 1: The Five Most Essential Terms

Term	Greek	Pronunciation	Meaning in Brief
Tetelestai	τετέλεσται	teh-TEL-es-tie	It is finished (and remains finished)
Metanoia	μετάνοια	meh-tah-NOY-ah	Transformation of perception
En Christō	ἐν χριστῷ	en khris-TOH	Your permanent location in Christ
Hamartia	ἁμαρτία	hah-mar-TEE-ah	Missing the mark of true identity
Pistis	πίστις	PIS-tis	Christ's faithfulness in you

Section 2: Additional Greek Terms (Alphabetical)

Term	Greek	Pronunciation	Meaning in Brief
Agape	ἀγάπη	ah-GAH-pay	Unconditional divine love
Aionios	αἰώνιος	eye-OH-nee-os	Age-pertaining (not "eternal")
Aletheia	ἀλήθεια	ah-LAY-thay-ah	Unveiled reality, un-hiddenness
Ananeousthai	ἀνανεοῦσθαι	ah-nah-NEH-oo-sthai	The renewed mind (passive — being renewed)
Anastasis	ἀνάστασις	ah-NAH-stah-sis	Standing up again, resurrection
Anōthen	ἄνωθεν	AH-noh-then	From above / born from above (not "again")
Apokatastasis	ἀποκατάστασις	ah-poh-kah-TAH-stah-sis	Restoration of all things
Apollumi	ἀπόλλυμι	ah-POL-loo-mee	To be lost, to miss purpose
Apolutrosis	ἀπολύτρωσις	ah-poh-LOO-troh-sis	Release, redemption — recovering what was always God's
Charis	χάρις	KHAH-ris	Grace as empowering presence
Dikaiosune	δικαιοσύνη	dih-kay-oh-SOO-nay	Right-standing (already established)
Dunamis	δύναμις	DOO-nah-mis	Inherent power, resurrection power

Section 2: Additional Greek Terms (Alphabetical) *continued*

Gehenna	γέεννα	geh-EN-nah	Valley of Hinnom (not "hell")
Hades	ᾅδης	HAY-deez	The unseen realm (temporary)
Hagios	ἅγιος	HAH-gee-os	Set apart, consecrated
Huiothesia	υἱοθεσία	hwee-oh-theh-SEE-ah	Coming of age as sons (not "adoption")
Kainos	καινός	kigh-NOS	New in nature/quality (not time)
Katallassō	καταλλάσσω	kah-tah-LAH-soh	Accomplished reconciliation
Term	**Greek**	**Pronunciation**	**Meaning in Brief**
Kolasis	κόλασις	KOH-lah-sis	Corrective pruning
Kosmos	κόσμος	KOS-mos	The world (scope of redemption)
Krino	κρίνω	KREE-noh	To separate/distinguish (not condemn)
Logos	λόγος	LOH-gos	Divine Word, organizing principle
Morphē	μορφή	mor-FAY	Essential form, true nature
Nous	νοῦς	noose	Mind, perception, consciousness
Pas	πᾶς	pahs	All, every, without exception
Perichoresis	περιχώρησις	peh-ree-koh-RAY-sis	Divine dance of the Trinity
Sarx	σάρξ	sarks	Flesh / false operating system
Sozo	σῴζω	SOH-zoh	To save, heal, make whole
Tartarus	ταρταρόω	TAR-tah-ros	Prison for fallen angels only
Teleios	τέλειος	TEH-lay-os	Complete, mature, fully developed
Theosis	θέωσις	theh-OH-sis	Participation in divine nature

Section 3: Core Awakening Concepts

Concept	Meaning in Brief
Awakening	Progressive recognition of what's always been true
Awakened Living	Daily life lived from union, not religious performance
Already/Awakening	Tension between completed reality and progressive recognition
Christ-Consciousness	Awareness of Christ AS your life, not just in your life
Divine Exchange	Christ took what was ours; we received what is His
Gift of Righteousness	Righteousness received as gift, not earned as reward
Gift vs. Reward Language	Receiving what's given vs. earning what's deserved
Righteousness-Consciousness	Living from identity, not for approval
Seated Position	Your current position with Christ in heavenly places
Union Reality	Your inseparable oneness with Christ
Universal Inclusion	Everyone already included—just unaware
Universal Reconciliation	God's accomplished reconciliation of the entire cosmos

Contrasts at a Glance

The vocabulary shift that changes everything

Greek Word Contrasts

Traditional Vocabulary	Awakening Vocabulary
Finished = completed event	Tetelestai = finished and remains forever finished
In Christ = metaphor	En Christō = permanent location/position (164+ times)
Repent = feel sorry, change behavior	Metanoia = transformation of perception
Sin = moral failure, rebellion	Hamartia = missing the mark of true identity
Faith = your effort to believe	Pistis = Christ's faithfulness in you
Righteousness = perfection to achieve	Dikaiosune = identity already established
Grace = unmerited favor	Charis = God's empowering presence
Truth = correct information	Aletheia = unveiled reality, un-hiddenness
Power = strength to try harder	Dunamis = resurrection power already in you
Eternal = endless duration	Aionios = age-pertaining, quality of life
Punishment = retributive torment	Kolasis = corrective pruning
Judgment = condemnation	Krino = discernment, making things right
Hell = eternal torture	Gehenna/Hades = wasted life / temporary state
Adoption = orphans becoming children	Huiothesia = coming of age as sons
Salvation = fire insurance	Sozo = wholeness restoration
Perish = go to hell	Apollumi = live disconnected from purpose
Reconciliation = possible if you believe	Katallassō = already accomplished
Perfect = morally flawless	Teleios = complete, mature
Transformation = self-improvement	Morphē = unveiling your true form
Flesh = sinful body	Sarx = false operating system
Holy = morally pure	Hagios = set apart, belonging to God
New = recently made	Kainos = new in nature/quality
Word = speech, statement	Logos = divine organizing principle of reality
World = sinful place to escape	Kosmos = scope of God's love and redemption
Mind = intellect	Nous = perception, consciousness

Concept Contrasts

Traditional Thinking	Awakening Reality
Reward language (earning)	Gift language (receiving)
Sin-consciousness	Righteousness-consciousness
Striving toward God	Resting in union
Becoming something new	Awakening to who you've always been
Working FOR acceptance	Working FROM acceptance
Christ IN your life	Christ AS your life
Climbing toward God	Already seated with Christ
Separation as reality	Union as reality; separation as illusion
Activity determines identity	Identity determines activity

Welcome Home

We don't strive for union with God; we awaken to the union that has always existed. This shift in perception—this awakening—changes everything about how we live, love, and see ourselves and others. His home is in you, and your home is in Him.

As more awaken, the knowledge of His glory—His overwhelming goodness—will cover the earth as waters cover the sea. Not because God's glory will finally arrive, but because humanity will finally see what has always been: we live, move, and exist in an ocean of divine goodness.

Welcome to the journey of discovering what has always been yours.

You've spent years speaking the vocabulary of sin-consciousness, striving, and separation. That language shaped your reality. Now you're learning a new language—the language of completed redemption, union with Christ, and awakening to who you've always been.

The language of awakening creates the reality of awakening.

Remember: you are not learning new truths here. You are awakening to truths that have always been. You are not earning what you do not have—you are receiving what has already been given.

As pastor Trevor Meier often says, *"I used to tell people what to do. Now I tell people who they are—and set them free."* This directly illustrates that exact transition—from behavior modification to identity revelation.

Tetelestai. It is finished. Now live from it.

SECTION 1:
The Most Essential Terms

These five Greek words form the foundation of everything. Master these first:

1. **Tetelestai** — It is finished (and remains forever finished)
2. **Metanoia** — Transformation of perception
3. **En Christō** — Your permanent location in Christ
4. **Hamartia** — Missing the mark of your true identity
5. **Pistis** — Christ's faithfulness operating in you

TETELESTAI (τετέλεσται)

Strong's #5055 (from τελέω, teleō) **Sources:** BDAG; Louw-Nida; MSB

Traditional: "It is finished"

True Meaning: Perfect passive tense—finished and remains forever finished; completed action with permanent results. The perfect tense in Greek indicates an action completed in the past with results that continue permanently into the present.

Awakening Impact: Nothing to add, nothing to earn, nothing to complete. Christ's work is totally done. This is His final declaration from the cross (John 19:30)—redemption is completely finished AND remains forever finished.

In Practice: Live from completion, not toward it. When doubt comes, when religion demands performance, when you feel inadequate—declare: "Tetelestai—it is finished!" You are not trying to complete what Christ has already perfected.

See Also: Sozo, Dikaiosune, Teleios

METANOIA (μετάνοια)

Strong's #3341 Sources: BDAG; Louw-Nida; HELPS Word-studies; MSB

Traditional: "Repentance from sin" (behavioral change and remorse)

True Meaning: Complete transformation of perception—seeing reality correctly. From μετά (meta, "beyond/transformation") + νοῦς (nous, "mind/perception"). While lexicons emphasize "change of mind," the compound etymology reveals a fundamental shift in how you see reality—transformation of consciousness, not just behavior modification. The mechanism is co-knowing. Paul captures it in 2 Corinthians 3:18 — beholding Christ as in a mirror, we recognize every feature of His image reflected back in us. This is not effortful transformation — "if this is all God's doing" (MSB) — it is a daily unveiling. We do not strive our way into metanoia. We behold our way into it. And what we behold is not a distant ideal but our own face, already articulated in Him.

THE AWAKENING GLOSSARY

Awakening Impact: Not about behavior change but consciousness shift—from sin-consciousness to righteousness-consciousness, from orphan-thinking to son-thinking. You're not changing yourself; you're seeing yourself correctly for the first time.

In Practice: Stop trying to change yourself—start seeing yourself correctly. It's not about doing better; it's about seeing better. When you sin, don't primarily focus on behavior change; focus on identity restoration.

See Also: Aletheia, Righteousness-Consciousness, Awakening

EN CHRISTŌ (ἐν Χριστῷ)

Strong's #1722 (ἐν, en - preposition) **Sources:** BDAG; Louw-Nida; MSB

Traditional: "In Christ" (often understood metaphorically)

True Meaning: Permanent grammatical location/position—appears 164+ times in New Testament. The preposition ἐν (en) with the dative case indicates fixed location or position. This is not metaphorical language but locative grammar describing where you are positioned.

Awakening Impact: You've never been outside of Christ—this is your actual address. "In Christ" is not a theological metaphor; it's your permanent residence. Every believer's location is ἐν Χριστῷ.

In Practice: Your location is "In Christ"—live from this reality. Every morning declare: "I am ἐν Χριστῷ." When circumstances challenge you, remember your location: you're seated in heavenly places in Christ (Ephesians 2:6), not striving to reach them.

See Also: Union Reality, Seated Position, Christ-Consciousness

HAMARTIA (ἁμαρτία)

Strong's #266 Sources: BDAG; Louw-Nida; LSJ; MSB

Traditional: "Sin, moral failure, crime against God"

True Meaning: Missing who you truly are—identity confusion. Standard lexicons trace *hamartia* to the verb *hamartanō* ("to miss the mark"), as in an archer missing a target. Francois du Toit and some scholars suggest an additional etymological dimension: ἁ (*ha*, negative prefix) + μέρος (*meros*, "portion/part"), meaning "without one's allotted portion"—living disconnected from your intended design. Whether understood as "missing the mark" or "living without your allotted portion," the root concept is the same: sin is fundamentally about being out of sync with your true identity as God's image-bearer.

Awakening Impact: Sin is amnesia, not offense. You're not morally broken—you've temporarily forgotten who you are. Sin isn't primarily about what you do wrong; it's about living disconnected from who you truly are.

In Practice: Replace "I'm a sinner" with "I temporarily forgot I'm a beloved child." When you sin, remember your identity rather than feel guilty. You don't need more shame; you need more awareness of whose you are.

See Also: Morphē, Metanoia, Righteousness-Consciousness

PISTIS (πίστις)

Strong's #4102 Sources: BDAG; Louw-Nida; MSB

Traditional: "Human faith, your ability to believe"

True Meaning: Can mean both human faith AND Christ's faithfulness operating through us. In phrases like πίστις Χριστοῦ (*pistis Christou*), Greek grammar allows two interpretations: "faith IN Christ" (objective genitive) or "the faithfulness OF Christ" (subjective genitive). Most English translations and the majority of scholars render this as "faith in Christ." However, a significant scholarly minority (including Richard Hays and Douglas Campbell) argues many instances should be translated as "the faithfulness OF Christ"—emphasizing that our salvation rests on His faithfulness, not the strength of our believing. Both readings are grammatically valid; the awakening message finds profound significance in the latter.

Awakening Impact: Faith isn't primarily your work—it's Christ's faithfulness in you. While human faith is real and necessary, it's awakened and sustained by Christ's own faithfulness. You're not generating faith by trying harder; you're awakening to His faithfulness that already holds you.

In Practice: Stop straining to believe harder—rest in His faithfulness. It's not about how strong your faith is, but how faithful He is. You're not holding on to God; God is holding you.

See Also: Charis, Tetelestai

Alphabetically organized for easy reference.

AGAPE (ἀγάπη) — Unconditional Divine Love

Strong's #26 Sources: BDAG; Louw-Nida; MSB

Traditional: "God's love" or "Divine love"

True Meaning: Unconditional, self-giving divine love—God's very nature and essence. Distinguished from ἔρως (eros, romantic love) and φιλία (philia, brotherly love). Agape represents the highest form of love—unconditional, self-giving, and divine in nature.

Awakening Impact: Love isn't what God does—it's who God IS (1 John 4:8, 16). And because you're in Him, it's who you are too. You can't earn it, lose it, or deserve it.

In Practice: Receive love as gift, not wage. You are loved because you exist, not because you perform. Stop trying to earn what you already possess.

See Also: Union Reality, Charis

AIONIOS (αἰώνιος) — Of the Ages, Not Eternal

Strong's #166 Sources: BDAG; Louw-Nida; LSJ; MSB

Traditional: "Eternal, everlasting" (endless duration)

True Meaning: Age-pertaining, age-during; describes quality more than endless duration. From αἰών (aiōn), meaning "age, eon, period of time." While standard lexicons primarily translate as "eternal," the word's derivation from aiōn (age/eon) has led some scholars to emphasize its qualitative dimension—the character of God's eternal life—rather than merely quantitative endless duration.

Awakening Impact: Dismantles eternal torment theology—"eternal punishment" becomes "age-during correction." God's justice is restorative, not merely retributive.

In Practice: When you read "eternal" in Scripture, consider whether it's describing quality (God's kind of life) or duration (endless time). Often it's the character of divine life being offered, not merely its length.

See Also: Kolasis, Gehenna, Apokatastasis

ALETHEIA (ἀλήθεια) — Unveiled Reality

Strong's #225 Sources: BDAG; Louw-Nida; MSB

Traditional: "Truth (facts, correct information)"

True Meaning: Un-hiddenness, unveiled reality—from ἀ (*a*, negative prefix) + λήθη (*lēthē*, "concealment/forgetfulness"). Truth isn't just correct information; it's reality with the veil removed, what was hidden now made visible.

Awakening Impact: You don't learn truth—you awaken to it. Truth is revelation, not information. The truth that sets you free isn't new facts but unveiled reality—seeing what was always there but hidden.

In Practice: Stop seeking information and start receiving revelation. Ask not "What do I need to learn?" but "What has been hidden that needs to be unveiled?"

See Also: Metanoia, Apocalypse

ANANEOUSTHAI (ἀνανεοῦσθαι) — The Renewed Mind

Greek: ἀνανεοῦσθαι (*ananeosthai*) **Root:** *ana* (ἀνά) = upward, back to origin + *neoteros* (νεώτερος) = renovated, renewed **Form:** Present Passive Infinitive **Strong's:** Related to G365 (*ananeoo*)

Scripture: "Now it's time to be made new by every revelation that's been given to you." (Ephesians 4:23 TPT)

"Thus you are habitually renewed in your innermost mind. This will cause you to be completely rebooted in the way you think about yourself." (Ephesians 4:23 MSB)

Traditional Understanding: Renewal of the mind is something we must do—a command to think differently, work harder at positive thinking, memorize more Scripture, discipline our thoughts through effort.

Awakening Understanding: The Present Passive Infinitive reveals the truth: **you are being renewed—not commanded to renew yourself.** This is ongoing work happening *to* you, not work you manufacture. The prefix *ana* (upward) connects to *anōthen* (from above) in John 3:3—both point back to origin, back to source.

The Greek Matters:
- **Present Infinitive** = progressive aspect, ongoing action in progress
- **Passive voice** = the subject receives the action (God renews you)
- **Contrast with Aorist** = Aorist presents completed action; Present shows continuous unveiling

The Key Insight: Your spirit was never contaminated—just like the watermark in a paper note. The lost coin never lost its original inscription and image. It was the **mind** that was veiled by darkness. As the MSB commentary states: **"There is nothing wrong with our design or our redemption; we were thinking wrong."** (Francois du Toit, MSB)

How Renewal Happens: "This transformation happens in the spirit of your mind, awakened by truth on a much deeper level than mere intellectual or academic consent. We often thought that we had to get information to drop from the head to the heart; but it is the other way around." (MSB Commentary on Ephesians 4:23)

Jesus confirms: "When you believe that I am what the Scriptures are all about, then you will discover that you are what I am all about, and rivers of living waters will gush out of your innermost being" (John 7:37 MSB).

Connected to Ephesians 4:24: "Remain fully immersed in this God-shaped new person from above. You are created in the image and likeness of God. This is what righteousness and true holiness are all about." (Ephesians 4:24 MSB)

The verb *endusasthai* (ἐνδύσασθαι) is Aorist Middle Infinitive—**completed action.** You have already put on the new person. Now remain clothed in this reality.

The Awakening Connection:
- *Anōthen* (John 3:3) = born from above
- *Anagennaō* (1 Peter 1:3) = birthed again, rebooted to original design
- *Ananeosthai* (Ephesians 4:23) = habitually renewed upward

All three share the *ana* prefix—all three point back to origin. You were never given a *new* identity foreign to your design. You were **rebooted** to the identity you always had in Christ before the foundation of the world.

Practical Reality: You don't renew your mind by trying harder. You renew your mind by:
- Setting your focus on your co-seatedness with Christ (Ephesians 2:6)
- Pondering the truth about you as displayed in Christ
- Receiving revelation, not manufacturing effort
- Letting the truth flow from spirit to heart to mind

The renewal is passive. Your role is to position yourself to receive—to tune in to what's already broadcasting from your union with Christ.

See Also: Metanoia, Anōthen, Anagennaō, Metamorphoo

ANASTASIS (ἀνάστασις) — Standing Up Again

Strong's #386 Sources: BDAG; Louw-Nida; MSB

Traditional: "Resurrection (future event after death)"

True Meaning: Standing up again, restoration to original position. From ἀνά (*ana*, "up/again") + ἵστημι (*histēmi*, "to stand"). While certainly including future bodily resurrection, the word also carries present implications of being raised up, restored, and positioned correctly.

Awakening Impact: Resurrection isn't just future—it's present reality. You've already been raised with Christ (Colossians 3:1; Ephesians 2:6). You're living resurrection life now, not just waiting for it later.

In Practice: Live as someone already raised, not as someone waiting to be raised. Your resurrection life has already begun. Engage today's challenges from resurrection power, not human striving.

See Also: En Christō, Seated Position

ANŌTHEN (ἄνωθεν) — Born From Above

Strong's #509 Sources: BDAG; Louw-Nida; LSJ; MSB

Traditional: "Again, born again" — a second birth that happens after a decision to accept Christ; a conversion experience that creates spiritual life where none existed before.

True Meaning: From above, from the top, from the beginning, from the source. Composed of ἄνω (anō, "above, upward") + the suffix -then (indicating origin/source). BDAG lists its primary meaning as "from above" (used this way in John 3:31, 19:11, James 1:17, 3:15, 3:17). While it can mean "again" in certain contexts, in John 3:3 the directional meaning — "from above" — is primary, as confirmed by Jesus' own explanation in the verses that follow. As the MSB notes: "Here Jesus uses the word anouthen meaning from above — see James 1:17, every good and perfect gift comes anouthen [from above]" (John 3:3 MSB Commentary).

The Greek Matters:
- **John 3:3** — "No one would even be able to recognize anything as coming from God's domain unless they are born from above to begin with" (MSB). Not a second birth in sequence, but a different birth altogether.

- **John 3:4** — Nicodemus misunderstands. As Godet remarks (cited in MSB): "He does not understand the difference between a second beginning and a different beginning." His "second time" is not Jesus' "from above."

- **John 3:5-6** — Two births: water (womb, physical origin) and Spirit (from above, divine origin). "Whatever originates out of flesh is flesh; but what is sourced beyond flesh in Spirit, is spirit" (MSB).

- **John 3:7** — **The Plural Shift:** Jesus switches to *humin* (ὑμῖν) — plural. He's no longer speaking to one man. He's addressing all of humanity: "Don't be so surprised when I say to you [humanity - plural.] You couldn't get here in the flesh unless you got here from above" (MSB). Every human being who exists in the physical arrived from a spiritual origin. This is a universal declaration, not a private instruction.

- **John 1:13** — **The Foundation:** Before the Nicodemus conversation, John established the principle: "These are the ones who discover their genesis in God, beyond their natural conception. This is not about our blood lineage or whether we were a wanted- or unwanted-child; this is about our God-begotteness. We are not the invention of our parents... man began in God" (MSB). Birth from above isn't introduced in John 3 — it's unveiled. John established it in the prologue.

The Translation Problem: The King James Version's "born again" (1611) collapsed *anōthen* into a sequential, time-bound event — something that happens after a decision. This created centuries of theology built on a secondary meaning of the word. Most modern translations now include "from above" in footnotes (NIV, ESV, NASB), acknowledging the directional meaning. The MSB restores the primary meaning directly in the text.

Connected Words:
- *Anagennaō* (ἀναγεννάω, 1 Peter 1:3) = birthed again, rebooted to original design
- *Ananeosthai* (ἀνανεοῦσθαι, Ephesians 4:23) = habitually renewed upward
- All three share the ana prefix — all three point back to origin, back to source, back to above.

Awakening Impact: Jesus didn't tell Nicodemus to get born from above. He told him he couldn't be *here* unless he already *was* from above. Birth from above isn't an event you achieve at conversion — it's an origin you awaken to. You didn't begin in your mother's womb. You began in God. Awakening begins when you receive and acknowledge Jesus — not because receiving creates the reality, but because it opens your eyes to a reality that was always there.

In Practice: Stop telling people they need to "get born again" as if they're spiritually empty. Start telling them they need to wake up to a birth that already happened — from above, from God, before time. You are not the invention of your parents. Man began in God.

Foundational Reading: For the full theology of birth from above — including Jesus' conversation with Nicodemus, the distinction between physical birth (water/womb) and spiritual origin (Spirit/from above), the Greek Perfect Passive tense revealing you ARE spirit whether aware of it or not, and the role of the Holy Spirit as "The Great Awakener" who reveals union rather than creates it — see *Awakening: Restorative Metanoia*, Chapter 4: Metanoia: The Shift That Changes Everything, Section 4.2.

See Also: Anagennaō, Ananeosthai, Metanoia, Aletheia, En Christō

APOKATASTASIS (ἀποκατάστασις) — Restoration of All Things

Strong's #605 Sources: BDAG; Louw-Nida; LSJ

Traditional: (Rarely discussed in modern churches)

True Meaning: Restoration of all things to their original state. From ἀπό (*apo*, "back to origin") + καθίστημι (*kathistēmi*, "to set in order"). Restored means returning to original design—you can only restore what originally existed. There was an original design—Eden restored, not escaped. Used in Acts 3:21: "the time for the restoration of all things."

Awakening Impact: God's plan includes universal restoration. The early Church Fathers (Origen, Gregory of Nyssa, Clement of Alexandria) taught that God's redemptive purposes extend to all creation. Everything will be set right. You're not becoming something new—you're returning to who you always were.

Note: This interpretation, while held by significant early Church Fathers, remains a minority position in contemporary Western Christianity.

In Practice: Hope bigger. God's restoration plan is cosmic, not just personal. Nothing is beyond redemption. No one is beyond reach. You're not waiting to escape earth for heaven—you're watching Eden restored.

See Also: Katallassō, Apolutrosis, Universal Reconciliation, Aionios

APOLLUMI (ἀπόλλυμι) — Lost, Not Destroyed

Strong's #622 Sources: BDAG; Louw-Nida; MSB

Traditional: "Destroy, perish (go to hell)"

True Meaning: To lose, to be lost, to waste—like the "lost" sheep, "lost" coin, "lost" son in Luke 15. The word emphasizes being separated from purpose, not annihilated or tortured. This word is used for the prodigal son who "was lost" (Luke 15:24, 32) and in John 3:16 ("should not perish").

Awakening Impact: When God says He doesn't want any to "perish" (2 Pet. 3:9; John 3:16), He's not threatening eternal torture. He's expressing a Father's heart that doesn't want His children living lost to their magnificent purpose, blind to their identity, wasted in religion when designed for glory.

In Practice: You can be *apollumi* (perished/lost) while physically alive—missing the very reason you exist. Perishing = living disconnected from divine purpose (not hell). Salvation = awakening to who you've always been (not fire insurance). The contrast in John 3:16 isn't heaven vs. hell but lost vs. found, asleep vs. awake, wasted vs. fulfilled in divine purpose.

See Also: Sozo, Metanoia, Hamartia, Aionios

APOLUTROSIS (ἀπολύτρωσις) — Redemption as Recovery

Strong's #629 Sources: BDAG; Louw-Nida; MSB

Traditional: "Redemption (rescue from damnation, payment to satisfy God's wrath)"

True Meaning: Release, deliverance, setting free—recovering what already belonged to you. From ἀπό (*apo*, "from") + λύτρωσις (*lutrōsis*, "release, redemption"). Redeemed means prior ownership restored—you can only redeem what already belonged to you. God didn't purchase you from a stranger; He recovered what was always His.

Awakening Impact: You were never a commodity sold to Satan or held hostage by divine wrath. You were always God's—temporarily lost, now recovered. "You were redeemed... with the precious blood of Christ" (1 Peter 1:18-19 NIV). The cross wasn't a transaction with an angry deity; it was a Father recovering His own children.

In Practice: Stop seeing yourself as someone who was bought from an enemy. You were always His. Redemption is homecoming, not hostage negotiation. You belonged to God before the foundation of the world—redemption simply brought you back to what was always true.

See Also: Katallassō, Apokatastasis, Tetelestai

CHARIS (χάρις) — Grace as Empowering Presence

Strong's #5485 Sources: BDAG; Louw-Nida; MSB

Traditional: "Unmerited favor, getting what you don't deserve"

True Meaning: Divine influence on the heart—God's empowering presence and transforming power. While the basic lexical meaning emphasizes favor and gift, Christian theological tradition has understood grace not merely as unmerited favor but as God's empowering presence—divine influence that transforms believers.

Awakening Impact: Grace isn't just forgiveness—it's transformation power operating in you. Grace doesn't excuse sin—it empowers righteousness. It's not merely pardon; it's power.

In Practice: Receive grace as power, not just pardon. When you struggle with sin, don't try harder—receive grace. You're not under law (self-effort) but under grace (divine empowerment).

See Also: Dunamis, Pistis

DIKAIOSUNE (δικαιοσύνη) — Right-Standing Already Established

Strong's #1343 Sources: BDAG; Louw-Nida; MSB

Traditional: "Righteousness (moral perfection you must achieve)"

True Meaning: Right-standing with God—already established, not earned. In Pauline theology, particularly in passages like 2 Corinthians 5:21 and Romans 3:21-22, righteousness is presented not as self-achieved moral perfection but as a gift received through faith—the righteousness of Christ imputed to believers.

Awakening Impact: You ARE the righteousness of God in Christ (2 Cor. 5:21). This isn't borrowed righteousness or a legal fiction; it's your actual standing before God. Righteousness is your identity, not your goal.

In Practice: Stop trying to become righteous—be who you already are. Live FROM righteousness, not FOR it. When you sin, your righteousness doesn't decrease; you simply acted inconsistently with who you are.

See Also: Tetelestai, Righteousness-Consciousness

DUNAMIS (δύναμις) — Inherent Resurrection Power

Strong's #1411 Sources: BDAG; Louw-Nida; MSB

Traditional: "Power, might"

True Meaning: Inherent power, explosive ability—resurrection power. This refers to inherent power—power residing in a thing by virtue of its nature—the explosive, resurrection power of God. The power of God to bring revelation.**Awakening Impact:** The same power (*dunamis*) that raised Christ from the dead is at work in you (Ephesians 1:19-20). You don't need more power—you need to awaken to the power already resident within you.

In Practice: Stop asking for power you already possess. The resurrection power is IN you. Awaken to it, don't beg for it. Receive revelation and remember what has always been true.

See Also: Charis, Anastasis

GEHENNA (γέεννα) — Valley of Hinnom, Not Hell

Strong's #1067 Sources: BDAG; Louw-Nida; LSJ

Traditional: "Hell, eternal fiery punishment"

Actual Meaning: The Valley of Hinnom (Ge-Hinnom)—a literal garbage dump outside Jerusalem where fires burned continuously to consume refuse. Jesus used this well-known location as a metaphor for the consequences of living disconnected from one's purpose—a wasted life, not eternal torture.

Historical Context: This valley had a dark history (child sacrifice under kings Ahaz and Manasseh—2 Chronicles 28:3; 33:6) and later became Jerusalem's garbage dump where fires burned continuously and worms consumed what the fire didn't. Jesus used this vivid, familiar image to describe the destruction that comes from living contrary to your design.

Awakening Impact: Jesus wasn't threatening eternal torture—He was warning against wasted lives. "Gehenna" represented destruction of purpose, not endless conscious torment. It's about this-life consequences and ultimate purification, not post-mortem sadism.

Make no mistake: Jesus' Gehenna warnings are serious. A wasted life is a tragedy. Living contrary to your design produces real destruction—broken families, corrupted minds, damaged communities, squandered potential. The fire of consequence burns whether you believe in it or not. Awakening theology doesn't minimize this; it clarifies what we're being warned about. The stakes aren't arbitrary punishment—they're the real destruction that comes from living disconnected from your identity and purpose.

In Practice: When you read "hell" (gehenna) in the Gospels, remember Jesus is using a physical location His audience knew well. The warning isn't "believe or burn forever" but "live according to your design or experience the destruction of a wasted life."

See Also: Hades, Kolasis, Aionios

HADES (ᾅδης) — The Unseen Realm

Strong's #86 Sources: BDAG; Louw-Nida; LSJ

Traditional: "Hell, eternal punishment"

Actual Meaning: The unseen realm, the grave, the temporary state of the dead. From Greek *a-* (not) + *idein* (to see), literally "the unseen place."

Lexical Definition: "The unseen realm; the place of departed spirits; temporary, not eternal" (BDAG, LSJ).

Key Distinction from Gehenna:
- **Gehenna:** Physical location (garbage dump), metaphor for wasted life
- **Hades:** Temporary realm of the dead, the grave, the unseen

Biblical Context:

- In Luke 16 (rich man and Lazarus), *hades* is a temporary holding place, not eternal torment
- Acts 2:27, 31 (NIV) - Jesus went to hades but wasn't abandoned there (resurrection)
- 1 Corinthians 15:55 (NIV) - "Where, O death, is your victory? Where, O death, is your sting?"
- Revelation 1:18 (NIV) - Jesus holds the keys of death and hades

Critical Revelation 20:14 (NIV): "Then death and Hades were thrown into the lake of fire. The lake of fire is the second death."

If hades *were* the lake of fire (eternal hell), this verse would be nonsensical. You can't throw something into itself. Hades is temporary; it gets destroyed. Death itself dies. The unseen realm is swallowed up.

Awakening Impact: Hades is not eternal punishment—it's a temporary state that will ultimately be abolished. Death doesn't have the final word. Even death and the grave are defeated and destroyed. Nothing and no one is permanently lost in the unseen realm.

The Lake of Fire: Rather than a torture chamber, the "lake of fire" in Revelation is better understood as God's purifying presence that consumes everything unlike Himself—death, hades, sin, false accusation. "For our God is a consuming fire" (Hebrews 12:29, NIV)—not to torture, but to purify. Notice what gets thrown into the lake of fire: death and hades themselves (Rev 20:14). Evil ceases to exist. The fire doesn't eternally preserve evil for torment—it annihilates everything that opposes life. God's judgment may finally remove what persistently resists healing, while His love continues to expose lies until restoration occurs. In both cases, wrath is the outworking of love against what destroys life.

In Practice: Stop fearing death as entry into eternal torment. Hades is temporary, and even death itself will be destroyed. The worst that can happen is not eternal torture but temporary disconnection—and even that is being redeemed. God's plan doesn't end with people in hades; it ends with death and hades themselves destroyed.

Note on Dual Application: The etymology of Hades (*ha-/a-* "not" + *eidō* "to see") yields two complementary applications in Scripture. **Cosmologically**, Hades refers to "the unseen realm"—the grave, the temporary state of the dead that will ultimately be destroyed (Revelation 20:14). **Metaphorically**, in Matthew 16:18 where Jesus builds His ekklesia on identity revelation, "the gates of Hades" refers to "the state of not seeing"—the blindfold of forgotten identity. Jesus declared that this blindfold mode will not prevail against those who have awakened to see who He is and who they are. Both applications flow from the same root meaning and both are defeated in Christ: the unseen realm will be destroyed, and the blindfold cannot overcome those who have received revelation.

See Also: Gehenna, Kolasis, Apollumi, Lake of Fire

HAGIOS (ἅγιος) — Set Apart, Already Holy

Strong's #40 Sources: BDAG; Louw-Nida; MSB

Traditional: "Holy (morally perfect, set apart for religious purposes)"

True Meaning: Set apart, consecrated, belonging to God. The emphasis is on being dedicated to God and His purposes. In Paul's letters, believers are regularly called *hagioi* ("saints" or "holy ones")—this represents positional holiness rather than merely behavioral holiness.

Awakening Impact: Holiness is your birthright, not your goal. You ARE holy through Christ—set apart, consecrated, belonging to God. This isn't something you achieve through religious effort; it's who you are by virtue of being in Christ.

In Practice: You're not becoming holy through effort—you ARE holy. Live from your set-apart identity. When you sin, you're not losing your holiness; you're acting inconsistently with who you are.

See Also: Dikaiosune, En Christō

HUIOTHESIA (υἱοθεσία) — Coming of Age as Sons
Strong's #5206 Sources: BDAG; Louw-Nida; MSB

Traditional: "Adoption—becoming a child of God; orphans adopted into God's family"

True Meaning: "Coming of age" as a son—stepping into the full rights and inheritance of sonship already possessed; like a Jewish Bar Mitzvah. While standard lexicons consistently translate as "adoption," some scholars (including N.T. Wright) have proposed that in the Roman context, this term could also refer to a legal ceremony recognizing a son's full inheritance rights—similar to "coming of age." Both interpretations emphasize the security and fullness of our identity as God's children.

Awakening Impact: You don't become a son/daughter—you awaken to the sonship that's always been yours. The Spirit seals your existing identity, not creates it. "Sonship is not for sale."

In Practice: Stop trying to earn sonship through performance. You were found in Christ BEFORE you were lost in Adam. Your origin is God, not your parents. Live from your birthright, not for it.

Note: The "coming of age" interpretation, while supported by some reputable scholars, remains a minority position.

See Also: En Christō, Pistis, Charis, Metanoia

KAINOS (καινός) — New in Nature, Not in Time
Strong's #2537 Sources: BDAG; Louw-Nida; MSB

Traditional: "New" (often confused with *neos*)

True Meaning: New in nature, quality, or kind—transformed from the inside out. Greek distinguishes between *kainos* (new in quality or nature) and *neos* (new in time, recently made). When Paul declares "if anyone is in Christ, the new (*kainos*) creation has come" (2 Cor. 5:17), he's not saying you're a recently manufactured product—he's declaring you've been transformed in your very essence.

Awakening Impact: The "new creation" isn't just spiritual—it's a transformation of your entire being. You're not a patched-up version of the old; you're qualitatively different. This *kainos* reality means your identity has fundamentally shifted. The old operating system of separation-consciousness has been replaced with union-consciousness. Science is now discovering that what we focus on literally rewires our brain and shifts gene expression—metanoia doesn't just change your thinking; it changes your brain wiring, your biochemistry, and your physical reality. When we align with the truth of who we are in Christ, our entire being functions as originally designed.

In Practice: Stop trying to improve the old—live from the new. You're not becoming a new creation; you already are one. The transformation isn't future—it's present reality waiting to be lived from. When old patterns surface, remember: that's not who you are anymore. You're *kainos*—new in nature, not just in time.

See Also: Metanoia, Morphē, Anastasis

THE AWAKENING GLOSSARY

KATALLASSŌ (καταλλάσσω) — Accomplished Reconciliation

Strong's #2644 Sources: BDAG; Louw-Nida; MSB

Traditional: "To reconcile (future or conditional)"

True Meaning: Complete exchange—already accomplished reconciliation. Reconciled means prior connection restored—you can only reconcile with someone you were first connected to. From κατά (*kata*, intensive) + ἀλλάσσω (*allassō*, "to change, exchange"), suggesting a complete exchange or transformation. In 2 Corinthians 5:19, the context indicates a completed action.

Awakening Impact: The world IS reconciled, not waiting to be. "God was reconciling the world to Himself in Christ, not counting people's sins against them" (2 Cor 5:19 NIV)—not punishment, not wrath, not counting. God has already accomplished the exchange—trading humanity's sin for Christ's righteousness. Reconciliation is an accomplished fact that people need to awaken to, not a future possibility they must achieve.

In Practice: See everyone as already reconciled, just unaware. Your job: awaken them to it. You're an ambassador announcing good news, not negotiating a possible treaty.

See Also: Kosmos, Tetelestai, Universal Reconciliation

KOLASIS (κόλασις) — Corrective Pruning

Strong's #2851 Sources: BDAG; Louw-Nida; Classical Greek usage

Traditional: "Eternal punishment, torment"

True Meaning: Correction, pruning—like gardener pruning a tree for growth. In classical Greek, *kolasis* was specifically distinguished from *timōria* (retributive punishment): *kolasis* was corrective (for the benefit of the one being corrected), while *timōria* was punitive (for the satisfaction of the one punishing).

Classical Distinction (Aristotle, Rhetoric 1.10.17):
- *Kolasis*: "inflicted in the interest of the sufferer"
- *Timōria*: "inflicted in the interest of him who inflicts it"

Awakening Impact: In Matthew 25:46, "eternal punishment" (*kolasis aiōnios*) is better understood as "age-during correction"—discipline for restoration, not torture without end. God's justice serves redemptive purposes.

In Practice: When you read "punishment" in Scripture, remember God's discipline is always corrective, never merely punitive. Even divine judgment serves restoration, not destruction.

This doesn't mean consequences are light. Corrective pruning hurts. A gardener cuts away dead branches—and the cutting is real. God's discipline is "painful rather than pleasant" in the moment (Hebrews 12:11 NIV). The difference isn't severity; it's *purpose*. Punitive justice says, "You broke the rules; now suffer." Restorative justice says, "You're destroying yourself; let me cut away what's killing you." Both involve pain. Only one leads to life.

What Gets Destroyed: God's fire doesn't destroy *people*—it destroys what destroys people. The lake of fire consumes death, hades, sin, lies, and false accusation (Revelation 20:14; 21:8). Evil itself ceases to exist.

What cannot be healed is finally removed—not the beloved, but the blindness; not the person, but the prison. This is wrath as the outworking of love against everything that destroys life.

See Also: Aionios, Krino, Gehenna

KOSMOS (κόσμος) — The World God Loves

Strong's #2889 Sources: BDAG; Louw-Nida; MSB

Traditional: "The world (often viewed negatively—sinful system)"

True Meaning: The ordered creation, the world system, humanity. While *kosmos* can refer to the fallen world system, in key verses like John 3:16 and 2 Corinthians 5:19, it refers to the entire world of humanity—the scope of God's love and redemption.

Awakening Impact: God loves THE WORLD—not just the elect, not just believers, but the entire cosmos. "God was reconciling the world (*kosmos*) to himself" (2 Cor. 5:19). The scope of redemption is cosmic, not selective.

In Practice: See the world as God sees it—loved, reconciled, included. Your neighbor isn't outside God's love; they're unaware of it. The gospel isn't "God might love you if you believe" but "God already loves you—wake up to it."

See Also: Katallassō, Agape, Universal Reconciliation

KRINO (κρίνω) — To Discern, Not Condemn

Strong's #2919 Sources: BDAG; Louw-Nida; MSB

Traditional: "To judge, condemn"

True Meaning: To separate, distinguish, discern—making right judgments. The word carries the sense of separating things out for proper evaluation and making things right. Jesus came not to judge/condemn (*krinō*) but to save (John 3:17; 12:47).

Awakening Impact: While *krino* can mean "to condemn," its primary meaning is "to discern, separate, or make right." God's judgment is restorative, not merely retributive—separating truth from lies, light from darkness, reality from illusion. The cross was God's judgment—not on humanity but on sin, death, and the powers of darkness.

In Practice: See God's judgment as discernment and correction, not condemnation. When Scripture speaks of judgment, ask: "Is this about making things right or merely punishment?" Even 1 Corinthians 11:32 says, "When we are judged by the Lord, we are disciplined so that we will not be condemned with the world."

See Also: Katallassō, Kolasis

LOGOS (λόγος) — The Divine Word

Strong's #3056 Sources: BDAG; Louw-Nida; LSJ; MSB

Traditional: "Word, speech, statement"

True Meaning: The divine Word—the rational principle organizing all reality; the creative force through whom all things exist. To ancient Greek philosophers, *Logos* meant the rational principle organizing the cosmos—the "divine logic" making sense of reality. To Hebrew thinkers, God's *Word* was the creative force that spoke worlds into existence. John united both: Christ is the divine rationality behind all reality—not just a teacher or moral example, but the organizing principle of existence itself.

Awakening Impact: John 1:1 declares that "in the beginning was the *Logos*"—face to face with God, mirroring the Father. When the *Logos* became flesh (John 1:14), that same face-to-face reality became your reality. The *Logos* is your source—you trace your origin to Him alone. This is why natural laws operate consistently (Christ is unchanging), the universe follows logical patterns (Christ is rational intelligence), mathematics describes physical reality (Christ's logic structures creation), and beauty exists rather than chaos (Christ's nature is beautiful). When Einstein marveled at the "unreasonable effectiveness of mathematics," he was glimpsing Christ's fingerprints on creation.

In Practice: Recognize that the same *Logos* who structured the cosmos has authored your story with equal intentionality. Nothing in your life is random. The same Designer who fine-tuned the universe governs the details of your circumstances. When you read Scripture, you're not reading as an outsider—you're reading the revelation of who you've always been, created in His image, face to face with the Father.

See Also: Aletheia, En Christō, Tetelestai

MORPHĒ / METAMORPHĒ (μορφή / μεταμορφή) — True Form Unveiled

Strong's #3444 (*morphē*), **#3339** (*metamorphoō* - verb form) **Sources:** BDAG; Louw-Nida; MSB

Traditional: "Form, transformation"

True Meaning: With form / transformed into true form. *Morphē* means "form, shape," while *metamorphoō* (μετά + μορφή) means "to transform into true form." Used in Romans 12:2 and 2 Corinthians 3:18 for the transforming work of the Spirit.

Awakening Impact: You're being transformed (*metamorphē*) into the image you already possess. This isn't about becoming something new but about unveiling what's always been true. Transformation is remembering your original form, not acquiring a new one.

In Practice: Transformation is remembering your original form, not becoming something new. Stop trying to create a new self—start unveiling your true self.

See Also: Hamartia, Metanoia

PAS (πᾶς, pas) — All, Every, Without Exception

Strong's #3956 Sources: BDAG; Louw-Nida; MSB

Traditional Reading: "All" often interpreted with qualifiers—"all *who believe*," "all *the elect*," "all *who respond correctly*"

True Meaning: The Greek *pas* means all, every, the whole—without exception. Scripture uses this word relentlessly to describe the scope of God's redemption.

Top 5 Key Scriptures (NIV):

- **John 12:32** — "And I, when I am lifted up from the earth, will draw *all* people to myself."
- **Romans 5:18** — "Just as one trespass resulted in condemnation for *all* people, so also one righteous act resulted in justification and life for *all* people."
- **1 Corinthians 15:22** — "For as in Adam *all* die, so in Christ *all* will be made alive."
- **Colossians 1:19-20** — "For God was pleased... through him to reconcile to himself *all* things, whether things on earth or things in heaven."
- **1 Timothy 4:10** — "We have put our hope in the living God, who is the Savior of *all* people, and especially of those who believe."

Other Key References to Explore: 2 Corinthians 5:19; Hebrews 2:9; 1 John 2:2; Romans 11:32; Philippians 2:9-11; Romans 8:19-21; Ephesians 1:10; 1 Timothy 2:4-6; Titus 2:11; Revelation 5:13

Awakening Impact: The same "all" that fell in Adam is the same "all" redeemed in Christ. The same "world" God loved is the same "world" He reconciled. Scripture adds no qualifiers—we do. ALL means ALL.

See Also: Universal Reconciliation, Katallassō, Apokatastasis

PERICHORESIS (περιχώρησις) — The Divine Dance

Not in Scripture - A theological term developed by the Cappadocian Fathers

Traditional: (Not commonly taught)

True Meaning: The divine dance—mutual indwelling of Father, Son, and Holy Spirit; the eternal circle of love. From περί (*peri*, "around") + χωρέω (*chōreō*, "to make room, contain, dance"). Describes how Father, Son, and Holy Spirit dwell in and permeate one another while remaining distinct persons.

Awakening Impact: You're included in this eternal circle of divine love. John 14:20 - "You are in me, and I am in you." You participate in the very life of God—the eternal love exchange between Father, Son, and Spirit.

In Practice: You're not outside looking in—you're dancing in the trinitarian embrace. Your life is caught up in this divine dance.

See Also: Union Reality, En Christō, Agape

SARX (σάρξ) — Flesh / False Operating System

Strong's #4561 Sources: BDAG; Louw-Nida; MSB

Traditional: "Flesh, sinful nature (always negative)"

True Meaning: Physical flesh OR false operating system (context determines meaning)

Two Distinct Uses:
1. **Physical flesh** - your God-designed body (neutral/good, as in "one flesh" marriage, Genesis 2:24; John 1:14 "The Word became flesh")
2. **False operating system** - the mindset of living independent from God, self-reliance, the "old man" way of thinking (negative, as in Galatians 5:19-21 "works of the flesh")

The Romans 7 Problem: *"I do not do the good I want to do, but the evil I do not want to do — this I keep on doing." — Romans 7:19 (NIV)*

This isn't moral failure. It's a systems failure. Willpower applied to the wrong operating system only makes the wrong operating system more active. The shift isn't trying harder. It's switching systems.

"The mind governed by the flesh is death, but the mind governed by the Spirit is life and peace."
— Romans 8:6 (NIV)

You don't defeat sarx by fighting it. You starve it by living from your identity in Christ.

Awakening Impact: Your body isn't the problem—wrong thinking is. When Paul says "crucify the flesh," he's not talking about hating your body but about rejecting the false operating system of independence from God.

In Practice: Don't hate your body—renew your mind. The flesh that was crucified (Galatians 5:24) is the old operating system, not your physical form. Your body isn't evil. Your humanity isn't the problem.

See Also: Metanoia, Nous

SOZO (σῴζω) — Saved, Healed, Made Whole

Strong's #4982 Sources: BDAG; Louw-Nida; MSB

Traditional: "Save (from hell)"

True Meaning: To save, heal, deliver, make whole, restore to original design. This single Greek word is translated variously as "save," "heal," and "make whole" throughout the New Testament. It encompasses complete restoration—spiritual, physical, emotional, relational.

Awakening Impact: Salvation isn't fire insurance—it's wholeness restoration. When Jesus said "Your faith has saved you" to the woman healed of bleeding (Mark 5:34), He used the same word (*sozo*) as spiritual salvation. Salvation is holistic restoration to your original design.

In Practice: Expand your understanding of salvation beyond "going to heaven." Salvation is present wholeness, not just future destination. You're being *sozo'd*—made whole in every dimension of your being.

See Also: Tetelestai, Apollumi

TARTARUS (ταρταρόω) — Prison for Fallen Angels Only

Strong's #5020 Sources: BDAG; Louw-Nida; LSJ

Traditional: "Hell" (often confused with gehenna and hades)

Actual Meaning: Used only once in the New Testament (2 Peter 2:4), referring specifically to rebellious angels being "cast down to tartarus" (Greek verb *tartaroō*). In Greek mythology, Tartarus was a prison for defeated gods and titans, far below hades.

Biblical Usage (2 Peter 2:4, NIV): "For if God did not spare angels when they sinned, but sent them to hell [*tartarus*], putting them in chains of darkness to be held for judgment..."

Awakening Impact: This word applies specifically to fallen angels, not to humans. It's not "hell" for people. The English translation "hell" obscures that this is a completely different concept from gehenna or hades.

In Practice: This term isn't about you. It's about judgment on rebellious spiritual powers, not humans. Stop applying every "hell" verse to yourself—context matters.

See Also: Gehenna, Hades

TELEIOS (τέλειος) — Complete, Not Perfect

Strong's #5046 Sources: BDAG; Louw-Nida; MSB

Traditional: "Perfect (morally flawless)"

True Meaning: Complete, mature, fully developed—reaching intended purpose. From τέλος (*telos*, "end, goal, purpose"). The term means "wanting nothing necessary to completeness"—describing wholeness and maturity, not flawless moral perfection.

Awakening Impact: You're already complete in Christ—maturity is awakening to your completion. *Teleios* doesn't mean sinless perfection; it means reaching your intended design, being fully developed.

In Practice: Stop striving to become complete—start living from completion. Growth is unveiling, not acquiring. You're not trying to become *teleios*—you're maturing into the awareness of the completeness already yours in Christ.

See Also: Tetelestai, Morphē

THEOSIS (θέωσις) — Participation in Divine Nature

Not in Scripture - A patristic theological term meaning "deification"

Traditional: (Rarely taught in Western Christianity)

True Meaning: Participation in the divine nature—becoming by grace what God is by nature; "partakers of the divine nature" (2 Peter 1:4 - θείας κοινωνοὶ φύσεως). This does NOT mean becoming God in essence, but sharing in God's attributes, life, and energies while retaining human personhood.

Awakening Impact: You're not just forgiven sinners—you're awakening to union with God, participating in His divine nature and sharing His attributes and life. The goal isn't just heaven someday but awakening now to the divine life that union with Christ makes real. This isn't mysticism—it's the consistent teaching of the early Church Fathers.

In Practice: You share in God's life, nature, and energies. As Athanasius said: "God became human so that humans might become god" (On the Incarnation, 54:3) (not God in essence, but partakers of divine nature). As a branch shares the life of the vine, you share the life of God.

The early church fathers read this in the Greek and simply said what they saw.

Athanasius: "He was made man that we might be made God" (On the Incarnation, 54:3). Not pardoned. Not evacuated. Made partakers of divine nature itself.

Irenaeus: "The glory of God is the living man, and the life of man is the vision of God" (Against Heresies, IV.20.7). The goal was never escape. It was fullness — life to overflow (John 10:10).

Gregory of Nyssa: Christ "was transfused throughout our nature, in order that our nature might by this transfusion of the Divine become itself divine" (The Great Catechism). Not visiting from a distance. Permeating from within.

This was the gospel of the first thousand years. Not rescue from a burning hell that was never in the Greek. Awakening into union that was always true. Jesus was not God's emergency response plan. God's mind was made up before the foundation of the world (Ephesians 1:4 NIV). Jesus came to reveal what was always there — you were never outside Him.

As He is, so are we in this world (1 John 4:17 NIV). Now. Already.

That is the shift. Not from sin-consciousness to better behavior. From separation-consciousness to union-consciousness. From performing for a distant God to living from a God who transfused Himself into our nature so we would never be outside Him again.

The gospel was never an evacuation plan. It was always an awakening.

See Also: Incarnation, Hypostatic Union, Morphē, Perichoresis, Hagios

SECTION 3:
Core Awakening Concepts

Understanding the vocabulary of transformation

"Gift language puts reward language out of business." — Francois du Toit (MSB Commentary)

These concepts aren't abstract theology—they're practical realities that transform how you experience God, yourself, and daily life.

AWAKENING

Definition: The progressive recognition of what has always been true about your identity and union with Christ

Not: Becoming something new **But:** Recognizing who you've always been

Key Scriptures:
- **Ephesians 5:14 (NIV)** - "Wake up, sleeper, rise from the dead, and Christ will shine on you."
- **Romans 13:11 (NIV)** - "The hour has already come for you to wake up from your slumber."

What You're Awakening To:
- Your eternal union with Christ (never been separate)
- Your complete righteousness (already established)
- Your seated position (already in heavenly places)
- Your finished redemption (nothing left to earn)
- Your true identity (beloved child, not orphan)

Awakening Impact: Like dawn gradually reveals what was always there, you're progressively awakening to reality. You're not becoming righteous—you're awakening to your righteousness. You're not becoming God's child—you're awakening to the sonship that's always been yours.

In Practice: You're not climbing toward God—you're waking up IN God. The journey isn't from earth to heaven but from sleep to wakefulness.

See Also: Metanoia, Aletheia, Morphē

ALREADY / AWAKENING

Definition: The dynamic tension between what's already true (completed in Christ) and what we're progressively recognizing

Key Scripture: Philippians 3:12 (NIV) - "Not that I have already obtained all this, or have already arrived at my goal, but I press on to take hold of that for which Christ Jesus took hold of me."

The Balance: Everything you need is already yours in Christ (already), and you're progressively awakening to that reality (awakening). Growth isn't becoming something you're not—it's expressing what you already are.

Practical Examples:
- **Righteousness:** Already = You ARE righteous. Awakening = Learning to live FROM that gift
- **Healing:** Already = By His stripes you WERE healed. Awakening = Manifesting that gift now
- **Authority:** Already = Seated in heavenly places. Awakening = Learning to exercise that position
- **In Practice:** Stop striving to become what you already are. Awaken to the already, receive the gifts, and watch them manifest.

See Also: Tetelestai, Awakening, Charis

CHRIST-CONSCIOUSNESS

Definition: Constant awareness of Christ as your life, not just in your life—daily living from union, not religious performance

Key Scriptures:
- **Galatians 2:20 (NIV)** - "I have been crucified with Christ and I no longer live, but Christ lives in me."
- **Colossians 3:3-4 (NIV)** - "For you died, and your life is now hidden with Christ in God. When Christ, who is your life, appears, then you also will appear with him in glory."

The Shift:

Old	New
Christ IN your life (He helps you)	Christ AS your life (He lives AS you)
Activity determines identity	Identity determines activity

This isn't metaphor—it's mystical reality. Christ isn't just a helpful presence; He IS your life. This is a gift received at salvation, not earned through spiritual maturity.

In Practice: It's not you living for Him—it's Him living AS you. Don't pray to become spiritual—pray because you ARE spiritual. Don't serve to earn God's favor—serve because you already have it.

See Also: Union Reality, En Christō, Perichoresis

CO-CRUCIFIXION / CO-RESURRECTION

Definition: Your participation in Christ's death and resurrection— already accomplished— you died WITH Him and were raised WITH Him

Key Scriptures:
- **Romans 6:6 (NIV)** - "Our old self was crucified with him."
- **Colossians 3:1 (NIV)** - "Since you have been raised with Christ, set your hearts on things above."

The Reality:
- Your old self DIED at the cross (past tense, completed)
- You WERE raised with Christ (past tense, completed)
- This isn't something you do—it's something that happened TO you

Awakening Impact: You're not trying to crucify your old self—it's already dead. You're not trying to rise with Christ—you've already been raised. Live from resurrection, not toward it.

In Practice: When old patterns arise: "That died at the cross—it's already dead." When shame attacks: "I died to that identity. I am new."

See Also: Anastasis, En Christō, Divine Exchange

DIVINE EXCHANGE

Definition: What happened at the cross—Christ took what was ours so we could receive what is His

Key Scripture: 2 Corinthians 5:21 (NIV) - "God made him who had no sin to be sin for us, so that in him we might become the righteousness of God."

The Exchange:
- He took our sin → We received His righteousness
- He took our curse → We received His blessing
- He took our death → We received His life
- He took our shame → We received His glory
- He took our rejection → We received His acceptance

This exchange wasn't a trade we negotiated; it was a gift He gave. We brought nothing but our need.

In Practice: When shame, condemnation, or inadequacy arise, remember the exchange: "He took that. I received this." Live from the fullness you've already received.

See Also: Tetelestai, Dikaiosune, Katallassō

RIGHTEOUSNESS-CONSCIOUSNESS

Definition: Living from your permanent right-standing with God—righteousness received as gift, not earned as reward

Key Scriptures:

- **Romans 5:17 (NIV)** - "Those who receive God's abundant provision of grace and of the gift of righteousness reign in life."
- **2 Corinthians 5:21 (NIV)** - "God made him who had no sin to be sin for us, so that in him we might become the righteousness of God."

The Shift:

Sin-Consciousness (Old)	Righteousness-Consciousness
Focused on failures	Focused on who you are in Christ
"I'm a sinner saved by grace"	"I'm the righteousness of God in Christ"
Reward-language: earn acceptance	Gift-language: receive what's given

Notice Paul calls righteousness a "gift"—not achievement, not reward. You don't work for gifts; you receive them.

Awakening Impact: When you sin, righteousness-consciousness doesn't deny it—it addresses it from a different foundation. Instead of "I must earn my way back," you declare: "That doesn't match who I am."

In Practice: Start each day declaring who you ARE. When you sin, don't earn righteousness back—receive the gift that never left.

See Also: Dikaiosune, Charis, Metanoia

SEATED POSITION

Definition: Your current position with Christ in heavenly places—already accomplished, not a future goal

Key Scripture: Ephesians 2:6 (NIV) - "God raised us up with Christ and seated us with him in the heavenly realms in Christ Jesus."

Notice the past tense: "seated us." Not "will seat." Already done. You didn't climb to this position; you were placed there. Gift, not reward.

Where You Are:

- **Seated** — Rest, not striving
- **With Christ** — United to Him
- **In heavenly places** — Realm of spiritual authority
- **Far above** — Above all opposing forces

In Practice: Rule and reign from rest, not striving. When problems arise, engage from your seated position (above), not from earth's perspective (beneath).

See Also: En Christō, Anastasis, Union Reality

UNION REALITY

Definition: The permanent, unbreakable oneness with Christ—you are organically joined to Him as one spirit

Key Scriptures:
- **1 Corinthians 6:17 (NIV)** - "Whoever is united with the Lord is one with him in spirit."
- **John 15:5 (NIV)** - "I am the vine; you are the branches."
- **Romans 8:38-39 (NIV)** - "Nothing in all creation will be able to separate us from the love of God."

Truth: You can't be "un-oned" from the One who holds all things together.

Your union with Christ isn't something you create through spiritual disciplines or earn through obedience—it's a gift you receive and awaken to.

Awakening Impact: You're not working toward union—you're living FROM union. Separation is the illusion; union is the reality. Even when you sin, you don't fall out of union—you act inconsistently with the union that remains constant.

In Practice: Stop trying to "get closer" to God—you're already one spirit with Him. Live from union, not toward it.

See Also: En Christō, Perichoresis, Christ-Consciousness

UNIVERSAL INCLUSION

Definition: All humanity included in Christ's redemptive work—not universalism but universal inclusion in Christ's singular work

Key Scripture: Ephesians 1:4 (NIV) - "He chose us in him before the creation of the world."
Humanity's inclusion in Christ isn't a reward earned by believing—it's a gift established before creation. Our inclusion preceded our awareness.

What It's NOT:
- ✗ Universalism (all paths lead to God)
- ✗ Automatic salvation without response
- ✗ License to sin

It is NOT minimizing the seriousness of sin. Awakening theology takes sin *more* seriously than traditional theology, not less. Here's why:
Traditional theology often reduces sin to rule-breaking that offends God and requires punishment. Awakening theology reveals sin as life-destruction—acting against your design in ways that waste your purpose, damage relationships, corrupt your perception, and produce real suffering.
Sowing and reaping is deadly serious. "Do not be deceived: God cannot be mocked. A man reaps what he sows" (Galatians 6:7 NIV). This isn't God imposing arbitrary consequences—it's reality's structure. Plant poison, harvest poison. The farmer who ignores gravity doesn't anger gravity; he breaks himself against it. Sin matters precisely because it destroys—not because it triggers divine wrath. A father who warns his

child away from fire isn't threatening punishment; he's describing reality. The fire burns whether the father is angry or not.

The consequences are real:
- Broken relationships don't mend themselves
- Wasted years don't return
- Damaged trust takes decades to rebuild
- Patterns of sin rewire the brain toward destruction
- Generational wounds cascade through families

Awakening theology doesn't say "sin doesn't matter." It says sin matters so much that God entered our condition to heal us from within—because behavior modification couldn't touch the depth of the damage.

What It IS:
- ✓ All humanity included in Christ's work
- ✓ Not all have awakened to their inclusion
- ✓ Christ is the singular path—and in Him, all are already found our "yes" awakens you to inclusion that was always there

The Two Adams: Romans 5:18 (NIV) - "Just as one trespass resulted in condemnation for all people, so also one righteous act resulted in justification and life for all people." The same "all" that fell in Adam is the same "all" redeemed in Christ.

In Practice: See every person as already included—just unaware. Your message: "You're already loved—wake up to it."

See Also: Katallassō, Universal Reconciliation, En Christō

UNIVERSAL RECONCILIATION

Key Greek Terms: Apolutrosis (redeemed), Katallassō (reconciled), Apokatastasis (restored)

Biblical Reality: God's accomplished redemption, reconciliation, and restoration of the entire cosmos

The Triad That Proves Prior Relationship:
- **Redeemed** — You can only redeem what already belonged to you
- **Reconciled** — You can only reconcile with someone you were first connected to
- **Restored** — You can only restore what originally existed

These words prove humanity was never foreign to God. We were His before we were lost.

Key Scriptures:
- **2 Corinthians 5:19 (NIV)** — "God was reconciling the world to himself in Christ, not counting people's sins against them."
- **Colossians 1:19-20 (NIV)** — "Through him to reconcile to himself all things, whether things on earth or things in heaven."
- **Acts 3:21 (NIV)** — "Heaven must receive him until the time comes for God to restore everything."

Note: This interpretation, while held by significant early Church Fathers (Origen, Gregory of Nyssa, Clement of Alexandria), remains a minority position in contemporary Western Christianity.

This Changes Everything:
- Prayer isn't reaching a distant God but communing with One in whom you live
- Holiness isn't getting closer to God but expressing union that already exists
- Mission isn't convincing God to love people but awakening them to love that's always been theirs

See Also: Apolutrosis, Katallassō, Apokatastasis, En Christō

SECTION 4:
Replacing Old Vocabulary with Truth

These aren't just theological errors—they're prison walls. Each keeps you working FOR what you've already been GIVEN.

ETERNAL CONSCIOUS TORMENT (ECT)

Foundational Reading: For the full theological case against ECT — including the Nicene Creed's conspicuous silence on eternal torment, the systematic mistranslation of *Sheol, Hades, Gehenna, Aionios,* and *Kolasis,* and how Augustine's Latin-based theology displaced the early Church Fathers' restorative understanding — see *Awakening: Restorative Metanoia,* Chapter 7: Rediscovering the Original Gospel (Part III), with supporting material in Chapters 9–11.

The Lie: Unbelievers burn forever in hell with no hope of redemption

The Truth: God's justice is restorative, not retributive; aiōnios means age-during correction, not endless torture

The Before-the-Foundation Problem:
Scripture reveals a redemption timeline that makes ECT internally incoherent:

(Before the Cross):
- **Revelation 13:8** — The Lamb was slain "before the foundation of the world"
- **Ephesians 1:4** — We were chosen IN HIM "before the creation of the world"
- **2 Timothy 1:9 — Grace was given us in Christ "before the beginning of time"**

(At the Cross):
- **John 1:29** — He takes away the sin of THE WORLD (not "some")
- **Colossians 1:20** — Through him to reconcile ALL THINGS to himself
- **2 Corinthians 5:19** — God was reconciling THE WORLD, NOT counting sins

If redemption was planned before creation and accomplished at the cross for ALL... how can billions be eternally excluded from what was finished before they were born?

The Completion Argument:
- **Colossians 1:19-20** — "For God was pleased to have all his fullness dwell in him, and through him to reconcile to himself ALL THINGS... by making peace through his blood."
- **Colossians 1:17** — "In him ALL THINGS hold together."
- **Ephesians 1:10** — "To bring UNITY TO ALL THINGS in heaven and on earth under Christ."

Everything finds completion in Him. ALL things. Not some things. Not most things. ALL.

The Father's Nature Argument:
ECT is incompatible with the revealed nature of our Father:
- **Good** — "Every good and perfect gift is from above" (James 1:17). Is eternal torture a "good gift"?

- **Perfect** — "Your Father in heaven is perfect" (Matthew 5:48 NIV). Does perfection create billions for endless suffering?

- **All-Powerful** — "Nothing is impossible with God" (Luke 1:37 NIV). Can He desire all to be saved yet lack power to accomplish it?

- **Loving** — 'God IS love' (1 John 4:8 NIV). Not 'has love' — IS love. And love keeps no record of wrongs (1 Corinthians 13:5). The Father gave all judgment to the Son (John 5:22) — the same Son who said 'I did not come to judge the world, but to save it' (John 12:47) and defined His mission as seeking and saving the lost (Luke 19:10 NIV). If you've seen Jesus, you've seen the Father (John 14:9). There is no hidden, angry God behind a merciful Son. The Judge IS the Seeker."

- **Sees the End from the Beginning** — "I make known the end from the beginning" (Isaiah 46:10 NIV). Did He create knowing most would suffer eternally?

A Father who sees the end from the beginning, creates humanity as His family, accomplishes redemption before creation, reconciles ALL things at the cross... and then eternally torments the majority of His children?

This isn't theology. It's contradiction.

The Scope Argument:
- **Romans 5:18** — "Just as one trespass resulted in condemnation for ALL people, so also one righteous act resulted in justification and life for ALL people."

- **1 Corinthians 15:22** — "As in Adam ALL die, so in Christ ALL will be made alive."

The scope of redemption must equal the scope of the fall. If "all" means all for Adam's sin, "all" must mean all for Christ's redemption.

Biblical Reality:
- **1 Timothy 2:4 (NIV)** — "God wants all people to be saved."

- **2 Peter 3:9 (NIV)** — "He is patient, not wanting anyone to perish."

- **Colossians 1:20 (NIV)** — "Through him to reconcile to himself all things."

- **Acts 3:21 (NIV)** — "Until the time comes for God to restore everything."

The Shift:
- **Old**: God's justice = endless punishment

- **New**: God's justice = correction that leads to restoration

A Balanced View: Two complementary perspectives help us understand God's restorative justice. One view emphasizes love exposing lies until restoration occurs—the fire purifies rather than punishes. Another view recognizes that judgment may finally remove what persistently resists healing—not as vindictive punishment, but as the necessary end of evil itself. Both agree: wrath is not God's emotional reaction but His faithfulness to truth, the outworking of love against everything that destroys life. Evil ceases to exist; people are restored.

In Practice: This isn't about removing urgency from the gospel—awakening to life NOW matters infinitely. It's about trusting that God's love is bigger than our theological systems, and that a redemption accomplished before creation cannot be smaller in scope than a fall that happened within it.

Replace With: Kolasis (corrective pruning), Aiōnios (age-during), Apokatastasis (restoration of all things)

SEPARATION THEOLOGY

The Lie: Your sin creates actual separation from God

The Truth: You've never been separated—only blind to His constant presence

Biblical Reality:
- **Romans 8:38-39 (NIV)** - "Nothing in all creation will be able to separate us from the love of God."
- **Acts 17:28 (NIV)** - "In him we live and move and have our being."

The Shift:
- **Old:** "My sin pushed God away; I must earn my way back"
- **New:** "My sin blinded me to God's presence; now I realign my perception"

In Practice: Confess to align your perception with reality, not to earn forgiveness you already have.

Replace With: Union Reality, En Christō

PERFORMANCE CHRISTIANITY

The Lie: Do more to be more; earn God's acceptance through spiritual disciplines

The Truth: You already ARE everything in Christ—disciplines help you remember, not achieve

Biblical Reality:
- **Ephesians 2:8-9 NIV (NIV)** - "It is by grace you have been saved... the gift of God—not by works."
- **Colossians 2:10 (NIV)** - "In Christ you have been brought to fullness."

The Shift:
- **Old:** "I must perform to earn God's love"
- **New:** "I am loved—now I express that love"

In Practice: Spiritual disciplines don't earn anything—they help you remember what's already true.

Replace With: Gift of Righteousness, Tetelestai, Charis

SINNER IDENTITY

The Lie: Your core identity is "sinner saved by grace"—fundamentally broken

The Truth: You ARE the righteousness of God in Christ—your core identity is righteous

Biblical Reality:

- 2 Corinthians 5:17 NIV (NIV) - "If anyone is in Christ, the new creation has come."
- 2 Corinthians 5:21 (NIV) - "In him we might become the righteousness of God."
- Colossians 1:22 (NIV) - "To present you holy in his sight, without blemish."

You WERE a sinner. Now you ARE righteous. When you sin, you're acting inconsistently with who you are, not revealing who you are.

The Shift:

- **Old:** "I'm a sinner; sin is who I am"
- **New:** "I'm the righteousness of God; sin is inconsistent with who I am"

Replace With: Righteousness-Consciousness, Dikaiosune, Kainos

THE AWAKENING

Remember:
- You're not learning new truths—you're awakening to truths that have always been
- You're not earning what you don't have—you're receiving what's already been given
- You're not becoming something new—you're recognizing who you've always been

Welcome to Your New Operating System

Old System (Reward-Language)	New System (Gift-Language)
Earn, achieve, deserve, perform, strive	Receive, awaken, express, rest, enjoy
Work FOR acceptance	Work FROM acceptance
You're separated, trying to get close	You're united, awakening to closeness
It's never finished	It's finished—now live from it

Gift language puts reward language out of business.

Tetelestai. It is finished. Now live from it.

APPENDICES
The Journey Continues

The Glossary taught you the Greek words. Now these four appendices show you what to do with them.

A Note on Translation Choice

Appendix A: 51 Key Awakening Scriptures — Verses for declaration, meditation, and identity. These aren't meant to be studied but spoken—read aloud over yourself, prayed, memorized, allowed to sink from head to heart.

Appendix B: Gospel Scripture Unveiled — A translation comparison showing how those Greek words appear (or get obscured) in your English Bible. Seven key passages. Two translations. The awakening message in sharp relief.

Appendix C: How Did We Miss This? — The historical journey from Greek to English. Why the Western church lost sight of these treasures—and why they're resurfacing now.

Appendix D: The Gospel of Awakening — Everything synthesized into six points. The recovered good news you can believe, inhabit, and share.

APPENDIX
51 Key Awakening Scriptures

These scriptures form the biblical foundation of the awakening message. They're not meant to be read once but to become meditation anchors that continually deepen your revelation of who you are in Christ. Consider reading one each morning, letting its truth settle into your heart throughout the day. Remember: these aren't promises to achieve but realities to awaken to.

A Note on Translation Choice

I've primarily used the NIV (New International Version) for these references to demonstrate that these awakening truths exist in plain sight within the most widely-read English Bible translation. You don't need a specialized translation to see these realities—they're right there in the Bible sitting on most church pews and bedside tables.

However, where the Mirror Study Bible (MSB) significantly illuminates the Greek meaning and awakening message, I've included expanded renderings alongside the NIV. These strategic additions reveal how translation choices shape our understanding of awakening—especially for concepts like union, identity, reconciliation, and the finished work.

Where the Greek illuminates deeper meaning, I've included the original term in brackets [like this] to connect you to the linguistic foundation explored throughout this book.

SECTION 1: Core Identity & Union Scriptures
Understanding who you already are in Christ

1. Genesis 1:26-27 (NIV) — Created in God's Image

NIV: *"Then God said, 'Let us make mankind in our image, in our likeness, so that they may rule over the fish in the sea and the birds in the sky, over the livestock and all the wild animals, and over all the creatures that move along the ground.' So God created mankind in his own image, in the image of God he created them; male and female he created them."*

Awakening Truth: Your image-bearing identity isn't something you achieved or earned—it's your original design. Before the fall, before sin, before religion, you were created as God's mirror image. This is who you've ALWAYS been.

Reflection: What if the fall didn't destroy God's image in you but only blinded you to it? How does recognizing that you were image-bearers BEFORE sin—and still are AFTER redemption—shift your understanding of salvation from transformation to restoration?

2. 2 Corinthians 3:18 (NIV) — The Mirror Transformation

NIV: *"And we all, who with unveiled faces contemplate the Lord's glory, are being transformed into his image with ever-increasing glory, which comes from the Lord, who is the Spirit."*

MSB: *"Now, we all, with new understanding, see ourselves in him as in a mirror. The days of window-shopping are over. In him every face is unveiled. In gazing with wonder at the likeness of Elohim displayed in human form, we suddenly realize that we are looking into a mirror, where every feature of their image, articulated in the Lord, is reflected within us. The Spirit of the Lord engineers this radical transformation; we are led from an inferior mindset to the revealed endorsement of our authentic identity. From the fading glory of our own doing, to the discovery of the most amazing reality, that we are God's glorious masterpiece!"*

Awakening Truth: We're not becoming something new; we're seeing what's always been true.

Reflection: When you look at Jesus, what if you're actually seeing your own true face reflected back? How would recognizing yourself as "God's glorious masterpiece" change how you see your flaws and failures?

3. John 1:14 (NIV) — The Word Became Flesh

NIV: *"The Word became flesh and made his dwelling among us. We have seen his glory, the glory of the one and only Son, who came from the Father, full of grace and truth."*

MSB: *"The Word became a human being and resided in us! We witnessed his glory, the glory of the Father's uniquely born Son, full of grace and the accurate communication of his eternal thoughts."*

Awakening Truth: The Incarnation wasn't God visiting earth—it was God permanently fusing divinity with humanity. When the Word became flesh, He didn't just dwell AMONG us but IN us, making separation impossible.

Reflection: The Greek word "eskenosen" (dwelt/tabernacled) means He pitched His tent in us, not just among us. If God permanently fused divinity with humanity in the Incarnation, what does this mean about the impossibility of separation between God and mankind?

4. Ephesians 2:6 (NIV) — Already Seated

NIV: *"And God raised us up with Christ and seated us with him in the heavenly realms in Christ Jesus."*

MSB: *"We are co-included in his resurrection. We are also co-elevated in his ascension to be equally present in the throne room of the heavenly realm where we are co-seated with him in his executive authority. We are fully represented in Christ Jesus."*

Awakening Truth: Your position is already established—awaken to where you already are.

Reflection: If you're already seated with Christ in heavenly places, what earthly circumstance still has the power to make you feel small or defeated? What would shift if you lived from your throne room position today?

5. Colossians 1:27 (NIV) — Christ In You

NIV: *"To them God has chosen to make known among the Gentiles the glorious riches of this mystery, which is Christ in you, the hope of glory."*

MSB: *"Within us, God is delighted to exhibit the priceless treasure of this glorious unveiling of Christ's indwelling in order that every person on the planet, whoever they are, may now come to the greatest discovery of all time and recognize Christ in them as in a mirror. He is the desire of the nations and completes their every expectation."*

Awakening Truth: The mystery hidden for ages: you were never separated from Him. Christ indwelling is not just hope—it's the mirror revelation of who you've always been.

Reflection: What if Christ in you isn't something you achieved through prayer but something you're discovering was always true? How does recognizing "Christ in you as in a mirror" transform your identity?

6. 2 Corinthians 5:16-17 (NIV) — New Creation Reality

NIV (v.16): "So from now on we regard no one from a worldly point of view. Though we once regarded Christ in this way, we do no longer."

NIV (v.17): "Therefore, if anyone is in Christ, the new creation has come: The old has gone, the new is here!"

MSB (v.16): "This is radical. From now on we refuse to focus on any person's outward circumstances; focus on the flesh-realm is no focus at all. Even if it once seemed valid to focus on Christ from a merely historic point of view, we now know that Christ is so much more than a page in history; he is the face of our redeemed innocence."

MSB (v.17): "Now, in the light of your co-inclusion in his death and resurrection, whoever you thought you were before, in Christ you are a brand new person. The old ways of seeing yourself and everyone else are over. Acquaint yourself with the new."

Awakening Truth: This isn't future promise—it's present reality waiting to be recognized. We no longer see anyone *kata sarka* (according to the flesh)—not ourselves, not others. The old lens is gone. The new way of seeing has come.

Reflection: The "if" in "if anyone is in Christ" isn't a condition—it's the conclusion of the gospel. You ARE a new creation. What old way of seeing yourself—or others—are you still clinging to instead of acquainting yourself with the new?

7. Galatians 2:20 (NIV) — Union Life

NIV: *"I have been crucified with Christ and I no longer live, but Christ lives in me. The life I now live in the body, I live by faith in the Son of God, who loved me and gave himself for me."*

MSB: *"So here I am dead and alive at the same time. I'm dead to the old me I was trying to be and alive to the real me which is Christ in me. Co-crucified, now co-alive. What a glorious entanglement. I was in him in his death; now I discover that he is infused in me, in my life. For the first time, I'm free to be me in my skin, immersed in his faith in our joint-sonship. He loves me and believes in me. He is God's gift to me."*

Awakening Truth: Your old identity died; you now awaken and live from Christ's life within.

Reflection: "Dead and alive at the same time"—what aspect of the "old me you were trying to be" are you still exhausting yourself attempting to maintain? What would freedom look like if you stopped trying and simply lived as "the real me which is Christ in me"?

8. 1 Corinthians 6:17 (NIV) — One Spirit

NIV: *"But whoever is united with the Lord is one with him in spirit."*

MSB: *"In our union with him we are one spirit with the Lord."*

Awakening Truth: You don't achieve union—you awaken to the union that already exists.

Reflection: If you are literally "one spirit" with the Lord—not two spirits close together, but ONE— how does this dissolve the sense of distance or separation you sometimes feel in prayer?

9. 1 John 4:17 (NIV) — As He Is

NIV: *"This is how love is made complete among us so that we will have confidence on the day of judgment: In this world we are like Jesus."*

MSB: *"So now, in our awakening to our joint inclusion in this love union, everything is perfect. Its completeness is not compromised in contradiction. Our confident conversation echoes this fellowship even in the face of crisis; because, as he is, so are we in this world - our lives are mirrored in him. We are as blameless in this life as Jesus is. This perfect love union is the source of our confidence whenever we face the scrutiny of contradiction."*

Awakening Truth: Not "as He was" or "as we will be"—but as He IS, so ARE we now.

Reflection: "As he is, so are we in this world"—present tense. What would change about how you approach today if you truly believed you are AS BLAMELESS as Jesus is right now?

SECTION 2: Transformation & Metanoia Scriptures
The shift from striving to seeing

10. Romans 12:2 (NIV) — Metanoia

NIV: *"Do not conform to the pattern of this world, but be transformed by the renewing of your mind. Then you will be able to test and approve what God's will is—his good, pleasing and perfect will."*

MSB: *"Do not allow current religious tradition to mold you into its pattern of reasoning. Like an inspired artist, give attention to the detail of God's desire to find expression in you. Become acquainted with perfection. To accommodate yourself to the delight and good pleasure of him will transform your thoughts afresh from within."*

Awakening Truth: Change your seeing, not your striving. Transformation comes through perception shift, inwardly transformed (awakened) by the unveiling of your renewed mind.

Reflection: Where has "current religious tradition" molded your thinking into patterns of performance and striving? What if transformation isn't about trying harder but about becoming "acquainted with perfection"—the perfection you already are in Christ?

11. Revelation 13:8 (NIV) — Lamb Slain Before Creation

NIV: *"All inhabitants of the earth will worship the beast—all whose names have not been written in the Lamb's book of life, the Lamb who was slain from the creation of the world."*

Awakening Truth: Redemption wasn't God's backup plan—it was eternal reality before time began. In God's eternal reality, redemption was complete before creation ("slain from the creation of the world"), then revealed in time through the historical crucifixion 2,000 years ago. The cross didn't change God's plan—it manifested His eternal purpose.

Reflection: If your redemption was complete before creation—before you sinned, before you were born, before time began—how does this demolish the lie that you need to earn or maintain your salvation?

12. John 1:29 (NIV& MSB) — Sin of the World Removed

NIV: *"The next day John saw Jesus coming toward him and said, 'Look, the Lamb of God, who takes away the sin of the world!'"*

MSB: *"The next day John saw Jesus approaching him, and declared: Behold the Lamb of God; this is the one who would lift the sin of the cosmos like an anchor from the sea floor, for mankind to sail free."*

Awakening Truth: Not "will take" but "takes away"—present, continuous action. The sin of the entire cosmos is actively being removed.

Reflection: The Greek word for "takes away" (airō) means to lift up like raising an anchor. What if sin isn't primarily your bad behavior but the anchor of false identity keeping you from sailing free? How does this shift your focus from behavior management to identity awakening?

SECTION 3: Freedom From Condemnation & Sin-Consciousness

Breaking free from guilt and shame

13. Romans 8:1 (NIV) — No Condemnation

NIV: *"Therefore, there is now no condemnation for those who are in Christ Jesus."*

MSB: *"There is therefore now no guilt; no sense of liability attracting penalty; no reason to be separated from God's opinion of you in Christ Jesus."*

Awakening Truth: Not "will be no condemnation" someday—there IS none. Now. Already. Finished. Sin-consciousness is the real enemy, not sin itself.

Reflection: If there is literally ZERO condemnation—not reduced condemnation, not conditional forgiveness, but NONE—why do you still live under the weight of guilt? What would shift if you believed God's opinion of you in Christ is completely untainted by your failures?

14. 1 John 3:19-21 (NIV) — When Your Heart Condemns You

NIV: *"This is how we know that we belong to the truth and how we set our hearts at rest in his presence: If our hearts condemn us, we know that God is greater than our hearts, and he knows everything. Dear friends, if our hearts do not condemn us, we have confidence before God."*

MSB: *"In this we know that our beingness is sourced in that which is really true about us; our doing good is not phoney or make-belief; this is who we are in God's sight. So, even if our own hearts would accuse us of not really being true to ourselves, God is greater than our hearts and he has the full picture. His knowledge of us is not compromised. Beloved, when we know what God knows to be true about us, then instead of condemning us, our hearts will endorse our innocence and free our conversation before God."*

Awakening Truth: Your heart condemns from below (*kataginōskō*—to know from a fallen mindset). God knows from above—and His knowledge is not compromised. When you know what God knows, your heart stops accusing and starts endorsing your innocence.

Reflection: Your heart accuses you based on performance. God's knowledge of you is based on Christ's finished work. Whose assessment will you believe—your condemning heart that knows from below, or the God who is greater than your heart and has the full picture?

SECTION 4: Chosen & Reconciled Scriptures

You were included before you believed

15. Ephesians 1:4 (NIV) — Chosen Before Time

NIV: *"For he chose us in him before the creation of the world to be holy and blameless in his sight."*

MSB: *"He associated us in Christ before the fall of the world. Jesus is God's mind made up about us. He always knew in his love that he would present us again face-to-face before him in blameless innocence."*

Awakening Truth: Your inclusion wasn't a response to your belief—it preceded creation itself.

Reflection: You were found in Christ BEFORE you were lost in Adam. If you were chosen before the fall—before sin even existed—how does this destroy the fear that you might somehow lose God's favor?

16. 2 Timothy 1:9 (NIV) — Grace Given Before Time Began

NIV: *"He has saved us and called us to a holy life—not because of anything we have done but because of his own purpose and grace. This grace was given us in Christ Jesus before the beginning of time."*

MSB: *"He rescued the integrity of our authentic identity and revealed that we have always been his own from the beginning, even before time was. This has nothing to do with anything we did to qualify or disqualify ourselves. We are not talking about religious good works or karma here. Jesus unveils grace to be the eternal intent of God. Grace celebrates our pre-creation innocence and now declares our redeemed union with God in Christ Jesus."*

(MSB Commentary: The word kaleō means to identify by name, to surname. The word ἴδιος idios means pertaining to oneself—mankind is God's own idea before any of us participated in any way.

The words πρὸ χρόνων αἰωνίων pro chronōn aioniōn: Paul speaks of God's mind made up about us before the ages—before calendar time existed, before the creation of the galaxies and constellations. Jesus defines it as, "Before Abraham was, I am."

What happened to us in Christ is according to God's eternal, prophetic purpose—the word πρόθεσις prothesis, pre-designed/prophetic purpose. In the Hebrew tradition the showbread [prothesis] pointed to the true bread from heaven—Jesus, the incarnate word—sustaining the life of our design. This is beautifully realized in the account of Jesus with the two from Emmaus: their hearts were burning with resonance while he opened the Scriptures to them, and then around the table, their eyes were opened to recognize him as the fulfillment of Scripture—their true meal incarnated within the tabernacle of their flesh! [Luke 24:27-31]

Mankind's union with God is the original thought that inspired creation. —Francois du Toit, MSB)

Awakening Truth: Your salvation and holy calling were not earned by anything you did—they were given to you in Christ Jesus before time itself began. Grace is not God's response to your need; grace is God's eternal intent revealed.

Reflection: If grace was given to you in Christ before the beginning of time—before you could do anything right or wrong—how does this destroy the performance-based mindset that still tries to earn what was already freely given?

17. 2 Corinthians 5:19 (NIV & MSB) — World Already Reconciled

NIV: *"That God was reconciling the world to himself in Christ, not counting people's sins against them. And he has committed to us the message of reconciliation."*

MSB: *"Jesus did not act independently of his Father. God was present in Christ when they reconciled the total cosmos to themselves. Deity and humanity embraced. God's act of reconciliation takes every other conclusion out of the equation! No amount of trespasses can match God's evaluation of the human race. Redeemed friendship is now announced from within us!"*

Awakening Truth: Reconciliation is complete; we're awakening to what's already accomplished.

Reflection: "Not counting people's sins against them"—past tense, finished action. If God isn't counting your sins against you, why are you? What would shift if you announced redeemed friendship from within instead of begging for acceptance from without?

18. Colossians 1:19–20 (NIV) — All Things Reconciled Through the Blood

NIV: *"For God was pleased to have all his fullness dwell in him, and through him to reconcile to himself all things, whether things on earth or things in heaven, by making peace through his blood, shed on the cross."*

MSB: *"God is fully at home in him. Jesus exhibits God's happy delight to be human. He initiated the reconciliation of all things to himself. Through the blood of the cross God restored the original harmony. His reign of peace now extends to every visible thing upon the earth as well as those invisible things which are in the heavenly realm."*

Awakening Truth: The blood of the cross achieved cosmic peace—reconciling ALL things, not some.

Reflection: "ALL things"—not "most things" or "some things." If the cross reconciled ALL things to God, what are you still trying to reconcile through your own effort?

SECTION 5: Identity as Sons/Daughters Scriptures

You're family, not servants. Allow God to reintroduce you to yourself.

19. Romans 8:15–16 (NIV) — Spirit of Sonship

NIV: *"The Spirit you received does not make you slaves, so that you live in fear again; rather, the Spirit you received brought about your adoption to sonship. And by him we cry, 'Abba, Father.' The Spirit himself testifies with our spirit that we are God's children."*

MSB: *"Slavery is such a poor substitute for sonship. They are opposites; the one leads forcefully through fear while sonship responds fondly to Abba Father. We are not slaves to a cruel taskmaster but gifted with the spirit of sonship; engaging the tender affection of Papa without any reserve."*

Awakening Truth: You're not an orphan earning love—you're a child living from love.

Reflection: Where are you still approaching God as a slave instead of a son/daughter? What would prayer look like if you engaged "the tender affection of Papa without any reserve"?

20. Galatians 4:6–7 (NIV) — No Longer Slaves

NIV: *"Because you are his sons, God sent the Spirit of his Son into our hearts, the Spirit who calls out, 'Abba, Father.' So you are no longer a slave, but God's child; and since you are his child, God has made you also an heir."*

MSB: *"To seal our sonship God has commissioned the Spirit of sonship to resonate the Abba echo in our hearts; and now, in our innermost being we recognize him as our true and very dear Father. Can you see how foolish it would be for a son to continue to live his life with a slave mentality? Your sonship qualifies you to immediately participate in all the wealth of God's inheritance which is yours because of Christ."*

Awakening Truth: Your inheritance isn't future—you're an heir now.

Reflection: How foolish would it be to keep living with a slave mentality when you're actually an heir? What aspect of God's inheritance are you failing to "immediately participate in" because you're still acting like a servant instead of a son?

21. 1 John 3:1 (NIV) — Children Now

NIV: *"See what great love the Father has lavished on us, that we should be called children of God! And that is what we are!"*

MSB: *"Consider the amazing love the Father lavished upon us; this is our defining moment: we began in the agapē of God - the engineer of the universe is our Father. So it's no wonder that the performance-based systems of this world just cannot see this. Because they do not recognize their origin in God, they feel indifferent towards anyone who does."*

Awakening Truth: You're not becoming God's child—you ARE one now.

Reflection: "We began in the agapē of God"—you didn't become His child through adoption; you

BEGAN in His love. How does recognizing this as your origin—not your achievement—free you from performance-based living?

SECTION 6: Living in Him Scriptures

You exist within Him, not separated from Him

22. Acts 17:28 (NIV) — Living in Him

NIV: *"For in him we live and move and have our being. As some of your own poets have said, 'We are his offspring.'"*

MSB: *"He is as present as you are! For 'In him we live and move and have our being'; I am quoting your own poets. 'We are indeed his offspring.'"*

Awakening Truth: You don't journey toward God—you exist within Him already.

Reflection: Like a fish in water, you live and move and have your being IN God. What would change about your spiritual life if you stopped trying to "get closer" to Someone you've never been outside of?

23. Colossians 3:3 (NIV) — Hidden Life

NIV: *"For you died, and your life is now hidden with Christ in God."*

MSB: *"Your union with his death broke the association with that world; see yourselves located in a fortress where your life is hidden with Christ in God."*

Awakening Truth: Your true life isn't separate from God—it's secured within Him.

Reflection: Your life is "hidden with Christ IN God"—like Russian nesting dolls. You in Christ, Christ in God. How does this image of being "located in a fortress" change your sense of security and identity?

24. John 14:20 (NIV) — The Day of Knowing

NIV: *"On that day you will realize that I am in my Father, and you are in me, and I am in you."*

MSB: *"In the unfolding of this day, you will know that we are in seamless union with one another. I am in my Father, you are in me and I am in you."*

Awakening Truth: The day of realization—when you finally see the union that always existed.

Reflection: Jesus in the Father, you in Jesus, Jesus in you—"seamless union." It's not your knowing that creates this union; your knowing simply awakens you to it. What shifts when you realize awakening isn't achieving but recognizing?

SECTION 7: Finished Work Scriptures

It is finished—nothing to earn

25. John 19:30 (NIV) — It Is Finished

NIV: *"When he had received the drink, Jesus said, 'It is finished.' With that, he bowed his head and gave up his spirit."*

MSB: *"When Jesus had taken the vinegar he said, It is finished. He then bowed his head and handed over the spirit."*

Awakening Truth: Everything necessary for your restoration is complete—nothing left to earn.

Commentary: *The word tetelestai communicates the final consummation of all things; everything is now concluded. The Perfect Passive Tense denotes an action which is completed in the past, but the effects of which are regarded as continuing into the present without end. Nothing that happens in time could possibly intercept this act of God's redemptive genius.*

Reflection: "Tetelestai"—it is finished and REMAINS finished. What are you still trying to finish that Jesus already completed? What would rest look like if you truly believed nothing could intercept God's finished work?

26. Hebrews 10:14 (NIV) — Made Perfect

NIV: *"For by one sacrifice he has made perfect forever those who are being made holy."*

MSB: *"By that one perfect sacrifice he has perfectly sanctified sinful mankind forever."*

Awakening Truth: You're already made perfect and holy as He is holy—complete while growing or awakening.

Reflection: "Made perfect forever" (past tense, permanent) while "being made holy" (present, progressive). You're complete yet awakening. How does this paradox free you from striving while inviting you into transformation?

27. Romans 6:11 (NIV) — Consider Yourself

NIV: *"In the same way, count yourselves dead to sin but alive to God in Christ Jesus."*

MSB: *"Make this reasoning your logical and habitual conclusion. Live your lives in the mirror-awareness of your union in Christ Jesus; in him you died to sin, and are now alive unto God. Sin-consciousness can never again feature in your future."*

Awakening Truth: It's not about making it true—it's about considering what IS true.

Reflection: The Greek word logitzomai means to continually and habitually make a calculation to which there can only be one logical conclusion. What if overcoming sin isn't about trying harder but about making your union with Christ your "logical and habitual conclusion"?

SECTION 8: Righteousness & Grace Scriptures

You ARE righteousness, not earning it

28. 2 Corinthians 5:21 (NIV) — Righteousness of God

NIV: *"God made him who had no sin to be sin for us, so that in him we might become the righteousness of God."*

MSB: *"This is the divine exchange: he who knew no sin embraced our perversion; he appeared to be without form; this was the mystery of God's prophetic poetry. He was disguised in our distorted image and marred with our iniquities; he took our sorrows, our pain and our shame and birthed his righteousness in us. He took our sins and we became his innocence."*

Awakening Truth: You're not wearing borrowed righteousness—you've BECOME righteousness.

Reflection: "We became his innocence"—not "we are working toward innocence" or "we are trying to maintain innocence." How does recognizing you've BECOME righteousness shift your approach to sin and failure?

29. Romans 5:17 (NIV) — Reigning in Life

NIV: *"For if, by the trespass of the one man, death reigned through that one man, how much more will those who receive God's abundant provision of grace and of the gift of righteousness reign in life through the one man, Jesus Christ!"*

MSB: *"Death no longer has the final say. Life rules. If the effect of one man's crash-landing engaged mankind in a death-dominated lifestyle how much more advantaged is the very same mankind now that they are the recipients of the boundless reservoirs of grace, empowering them to enjoy the dominion of life through the gift of righteousness because of that one man, Jesus Christ."*

Awakening Truth: You're designed to reign in life through grace, not strive under law.

Reflection: You are "the recipient of boundless reservoirs of grace"—not someone trying to qualify for grace. How would your day change if you lived as someone empowered to "enjoy the dominion of life" rather than survive the death-dominated lifestyle?

30. 1 Peter 1:19–20 (NIV) — Chosen Before Creation

NIV: *"But with the precious blood of Christ, a lamb without blemish or defect. He was chosen before the creation of the world, but was revealed in these last times for your sake."*

MSB: *"But you were redeemed with the priceless blood of Christ. He is the ultimate sacrifice; spotless and without blemish. Jesus completes the prophetic picture. He was always destined in God's prophetic thought; God knew even before the fall of the world order that his Son would be the Lamb, to be made manifest in these last days, because of you."*

Awakening Truth: The cross wasn't emergency response but eternal revelation. You are the reason Jesus died and was raised.

Reflection: "Because of you"—the Lamb was slain before the foundation of the world FOR YOU. How does knowing your redemption was God's eternal plan—not His backup plan—transform your sense of worth and value?

31. Colossians 2:9–10 (NIV) — Complete in Him

NIV: *"For in Christ all the fullness of the Deity lives in bodily form, and in Christ you have been brought to fullness."*

MSB: *"In him, all the fullness of Deity resides in a human body. He proves that human life is tailor-made for God. We are complete in him. Jesus mirrors our wholeness and endorses our true identity. He is I am in us."*

Awakening Truth: You lack nothing—you are already complete in Him.

Reflection: "We are complete in him"—present tense. What are you still seeking or striving for that you already possess in your completeness in Christ? What would shift if you celebrated completeness instead of chasing it?

SECTION 9: The Awakening Gospel in Declaration

32. Romans 5:18-19 (NIV) — One Man's Fall, One Man's Victory

NIV: *"Consequently, just as one trespass resulted in condemnation for all people, so also one righteous act resulted in justification and life for all people. For just as through the disobedience of the one man the many were made sinners, so also through the obedience of the one man the many will be made righteous."*

MSB: *"One man's mistake brought a death sentence to everyone. One man's perfect obedience brought life and restored righteousness to everyone! The disobedience of one exhibits mankind as sinners; the obedience of another exhibits mankind as righteous."*

Awakening Truth: If Adam's one act affected ALL humanity without their permission or participation, Christ's one act is equally—no, MORE—powerful and inclusive. The parallel is exact: one man's fall condemned all, one man's obedience justified all.

Reflection: You didn't choose to be "in Adam" and inherit his condemnation—it just was. How does this reveal that you also didn't need to choose to be "in Christ" to inherit His righteousness? If Adam's impact was automatic and universal, how much more is Christ's victory automatic and universal?

33. 1 Corinthians 15:22 (NIV) — All Died in Adam, All Made Alive in Christ

NIV: *"For as in Adam all die, so in Christ all will be made alive."*

MSB: *"Just as all died in Adam, so all will be made alive in Christ."*

Awakening Truth: The word "all" means ALL. Every person who died in Adam (which is everyone) is made alive in Christ (which is also everyone). This isn't conditional—it's parallel and complete.

Reflection: Notice the perfect symmetry: "as in Adam ALL die" = "in Christ ALL will be made alive." You were included in Adam's death without choosing it. How does this reveal you're included in Christ's life whether you realize it or not? What if awakening isn't getting into Christ but discovering you were never outside Him?

34. 1 Corinthians 1:30 (NIV) — In Christ By God's Doing

NIV: *"It is because of him that you are in Christ Jesus, who has become for us wisdom from God—that is, our righteousness, holiness and redemption."*

Awakening Truth: Your position in Christ isn't your achievement—it's God's doing. You didn't work your way in; you woke up to discover you were already there.

Reflection: "It is because of HIM that you are in Christ"—not because of your decision, your prayer, your faith, or your commitment. How does knowing you're in Christ "by God's doing" demolish religious pride and performance anxiety?

35. Ephesians 1:11 (NIV) — Predestined and Included

NIV: *"In him we were also chosen, having been predestined according to the plan of him who works out everything in conformity with the purpose of his will."*

Awakening Truth: God's plan has always included you. Your inclusion in Christ predates your existence, your choices, and your awareness. You're awakening to what He planned from eternity.

Reflection: If you were predestined and included according to God's eternal purpose, what role does your performance play in securing your position? How does this truth free you to rest in His purpose rather than strive to fulfill yours?

36. Romans 8:38–39 (NIV) — Nothing Can Separate

NIV: *"For I am convinced that neither death nor life, neither angels nor demons, neither the present nor the future, nor any powers, neither height nor depth, nor anything else in all creation, will be able to separate us from the love of God that is in Christ Jesus our Lord."*

Awakening Truth: Separation from God's love is impossible. You were never separated—only blind to union that always existed.

Reflection: "NOTHING can separate us"—not sin, not failure, not doubt, not death itself. If separation is impossible, what are you still afraid of losing? What freedom opens up when you realize you can't fall out of God's love?

37. Ephesians 1:4 (NIV) — Chosen Before the Fall

NIV: *"For he chose us in him before the creation of the world to be holy and blameless in his sight."*

MSB: *"He associated us in Christ before the fall of the world. Jesus is God's mind made up about us. He always knew in his love that he would present us again face-to-face before him in blameless innocence."*

Awakening Truth: You were not chosen after you believed — you were associated with Christ before the fall even happened. Your inclusion in Him predates everything that could disqualify you. "Holy and blameless" is not a destination you're working toward. It is how God has always seen you in Christ. This is your origin, not your achievement.

MSB Commentary: The Greek word *eklegō* (traditionally "elect" or "chosen") literally means to associate — from *ek* (origin/source) + *legō* (to relate, to link, to weave together). An inseparable association exists from before the foundation of the earth that locates and defines you in Christ. And where the NIV reads "before the creation of the world," Paul actually uses *kataballō* — the fall of the world. The implications of the fall are completely canceled. We were found in Christ before we were lost in Adam.

Reflection: You didn't work your way into Christ — God associated you with Him before time began, before anything existed to disqualify you. If your inclusion predates the fall itself, what does religion have left to threaten you with? What changes when you realize "holy and blameless" describes how God has always seen you — not where you're trying to arrive?

Key texts that dismantle separation, fear, and performance-based religion

38. Acts 10:28 (NIV) — No One Is Unclean

NIV: *"He said to them: 'You are well aware that it is against our law for a Jew to associate with or visit a Gentile. But God has shown me that I should not call anyone impure or unclean.'"*

Awakening Truth: God's verdict over humanity is inclusion, not exclusion. No person stands outside His embrace.

Reflection: What if the only thing "unclean" was your perception? How would this reshape how you see yourself—and everyone else?

39. John 12:32 (NIV) — Drawn by Love

NIV: *"And I, when I am lifted up from the earth, will draw all people to myself."*

MSB: *"When I am lifted up from the earth, I will draw all of mankind and every definition of judgment unto me."*

Commentary: *He would be lifted up on a cross, descend into the depths of our hell, then, according to the prophetic word in Hosea 6:2, after two days, the entire human race he represents, will be co-quickened and on the third day, be co-raised, out of the lowest parts of the earth and elevated to the highest heavens (Ephesians 4:8,9; See Also Ephesians 2:5,6 and Colossians 3:1-3). "All" includes all of mankind and every definition of judgment. The subject of the sentence, as from the previous verse, is the judgment of the world—thus the primary thought here is that in his death, Jesus would draw all judgment upon himself.*

Awakening Truth: The Greek word *helkō* [ἑλκύω] means "to pull, drag, or draw with irresistible force." Jesus initiates our awakening—not human willpower. He drew all judgment to Himself so we would be drawn to Him in love.

Reflection: If Christ is drawing all humanity, what striving can you let go of? What hope rises when salvation begins with Him, not you?

40. Hebrews 1:3 (NIV) — Exact Representation

NIV: *"The Son is the radiance of God's glory and the exact representation of his being, sustaining all things by his powerful word. After he had provided purification for sins, he sat down at the right hand of the Majesty in heaven."*

Awakening Truth: The Greek *charaktēr* [χαρακτήρ] means the precise imprint, the exact expression. If you've seen Jesus, you've seen the Father. No contradiction. No hidden, angry God behind a merciful Jesus.

Reflection: What old images of God collapse when Jesus fully defines His nature? What fear melts when God is as Christlike as Christ?

41. Romans 11:32 (NIV) — Mercy for All

NIV: *"For God has bound everyone over to disobedience so that he may have mercy on them all."*

MSB: *"In God's calculation the mass of mankind is trapped in unbelief. This qualifies all mankind for his mercy."*

Awakening Truth: God's final word over humanity is mercy—universal, relentless, and restorative. The purpose of exposing disobedience was never punishment but qualification for mercy.

Reflection: If mercy is God's intention for all, why fear being excluded? What would your life feel like if mercy, not judgment, framed every thought?

42. 1 Timothy 4:10 (NIV) — Saviour of All

NIV: *"That is why we labor and strive, because we have put our hope in the living God, who is the Savior of all people, and especially of those who believe."*

Awakening Truth: Jesus is the Saviour of ALL—believers simply awaken to what has always been true. Belief doesn't create salvation; belief recognizes it.

Reflection: How does your confidence grow when salvation is rooted in God's action, not human qualification? What pressure lifts when you realize awakening reveals rather than earns?

43. 2 Peter 1:4 (NIV) — Partakers of the Divine Nature

NIV: *"Through these he has given us his very great and precious promises, so that through them you may participate in the divine nature, having escaped the corruption in the world caused by evil desires."*

Awakening Truth: The Greek *koinōnoi theias physeōs* [κοινωνοὶ θείας φύσεως] means sharers in God's very nature. Union is not symbolic—it's participation. You don't just relate to God; you share His nature.

Reflection: What if spiritual growth is not climbing toward God but awakening to the divine nature already within? How does this shift your understanding of transformation?

44. Hebrews 2:9 (NIV) — Death for Everyone

NIV: *"But we do see Jesus, who was made lower than the angels for a little while, now crowned with glory and honor because he suffered death, so that by the grace of God he might taste death for everyone."*

MSB: *"But what is apparent, is Jesus. Let us then consider him in such a way, that we may clearly perceive what God is saying to mankind in him. In the death he suffered, he briefly descended to a seemingly less elevated place than Elohim, in order to taste the death of the entire human race, and in doing so, to fulfill the grace of God and be crowned again (as a man, representing all of mankind) with glory and highly esteemed honor."*

Awakening Truth: Christ's sacrificial love is universal in scope—no one stands outside His death or His life. He tasted death for the entire human race, representing all of mankind. "Everyone" means everyone.

Reflection: If Jesus tasted death for everyone—the entire human race—what fear of rejection or exclusion is left? How does this demolish the anxiety that you might somehow be the exception?

45. John 5:22 (NIV) — The Father Judges No One

NIV: *"Moreover, the Father judges no one, but has entrusted all judgment to the Son."*

Awakening Truth: Judgment is not the Father's posture toward humanity—His posture is revealed in Christ: restorative, not punitive. And the Son who judges is the same one who said, "I did not come to judge the world, but to save the world" (John 12:47 NIV).

⌣ **Reflection:** What anxiety loses power when the Father looks exactly like Jesus, who refuses to condemn? What if every image of an angry, distant God dissolves in this truth?

46. Luke 15:20 (NIV) — The Father Runs First

NIV: *"So he got up and went to his father. But while he was still a long way off, his father saw him and was filled with compassion for him; he ran to his son, threw his arms around him and kissed him."*

Awakening Truth: The Father's love does not wait for repentance—it initiates reconciliation. Before the son's confession, before his cleanup, before any change—the Father ran.

⌣ **Reflection:** What if God embraced you before confession, cleanup, or change? What does it do to your heart to know the Father was already running toward you while you were still "a long way off"?

47. 1 John 2:2 (NIV) — Propitiation for the Whole World

NIV: *"He is the atoning sacrifice for our sins, and not only for ours but also for the sins of the whole world."*

MSB: *"Jesus is our at-one-ment, he has reconciled us to himself and has taken our sins and distortions out of the equation. What he has accomplished is not to be seen as something that belongs to us exclusively; the same at-one-ment includes the entire cosmos."*

Commentary: *The word hilasmos [ἱλασμός] means to conciliate, to bring about atonement, from hileos, gracious, merciful. Also reminds one of the word hilaros, cheerful, joyous, hilarious.*

Awakening Truth: The scope of Christ's sacrifice is explicitly universal—"the entire cosmos," not just believers. Jesus didn't just make salvation possible for the world; He is the actual at-one-ment for all creation. Our sins and distortions have been taken "out of the equation."

⌣ **Reflection:** If Jesus is the at-one-ment for the entire cosmos—not potentially, but actually—what does this reveal about God's heart for every person you encounter? How does "the entire cosmos" reshape your understanding of who's included?

48. Philippians 2:10-11 (NIV) — Every Knee, Every Tongue

NIV: *"That at the name of Jesus every knee should bow, in heaven and on earth and under the earth, and every tongue acknowledge that Jesus Christ is Lord, to the glory of God the Father."*

MSB: *"What his name unveils will persuade every creature of their redemption. Every knee in heaven and upon the earth and under the earth shall bow in spontaneous worship."*

Commentary: *See Isaiah 45:23 (NIV) "My own life is the guarantee of my conviction, says the Lord, every knee shall freely bow to me in worship, and every tongue shall spontaneously speak from the same God-inspired source."*

Awakening Truth: This is not forced compliance or grudging submission—it is spontaneous worship. Every creature will be persuaded of their redemption. This is what happens when truth is finally, fully, irresistibly seen—not coercion, but clarity.

Reflection: What changes when you realize "every knee will bow" describes not coerced submission but spontaneous recognition of love? What hope rises when you see this as the ultimate awakening of all creation?

49. 1 Corinthians 15:28 (NIV) — God All in All

NIV: *"When he has done this, then the Son himself will be made subject to him who put everything under him, so that God may be all in all."*

Awakening Truth: This is the ultimate goal of cosmic restoration—God being "all in all" [*panta en pasin*]. Not all in some. Not all in the elect. ALL in ALL. This is the final destination of redemption: complete union, total restoration, nothing outside His embrace.

Reflection: If God's ultimate purpose is to be "all in all," what does this reveal about the scope of His victory? How does this final picture reshape your understanding of who and what is included in God's restoration?

50. Acts 3:21 (NIV) — Restoration of All Things

NIV: *"Heaven must receive him until the time comes for God to restore everything, as he promised long ago through his holy prophets."*

MSB: *"Jesus is the theme of God's conversation, from the earliest ages; through the lips of the prophets who carried the Messiah in the womb of their words. He was to be held all along in the unseen heavenly realm for a time such as this. He is the restoration of all things."*

Commentary: *The idea of restoration was part and parcel of the Messianic expectation. The noun apokatastaseos [ἀποκαταστάσεως] comes from the verb apokatastēsei, meaning to restore to its natural and original condition. As a technical medical term, it denotes complete restoration of health; the restoring to its place of a dislocated joint.*

Awakening Truth: The Greek *apokatastasis pantōn* [ἀποκατάστασις πάντων] means "restoration of ALL things"—not some things, not most things, but everything restored to its natural and original condition. Like a dislocated joint being set back in place, God is restoring all creation to its intended design.

Reflection: If God's plan has always been to "restore everything" to its original condition, what situation or person have you considered beyond restoration? How does *apokatastasis* expand your hope for creation's future—and your own?

AND NOW... THE 51ˢᵗ SCRIPTURE

We've journeyed through identity and union. We've demolished religion and awakened to grace. We've discovered we were chosen before creation, seated in heavenly places, one spirit with Him, reconciled before we believed, and loved with a love from which nothing can separate us.

But where does it all lead?

Every awakening scripture has been pointing to one destination. Every truth about who you are has been guiding you to one place. Every revelation of finished work, every unveiling of union, every demolition of separation theology has been preparing you for this:

You're not just saved. You're not just forgiven. You're not just accepted.

You're HOME.

51. John 14:2 (NIV) — You Make The Father's House A Home

NIV: *"My Father's house has many rooms; if that were not so, would I have told you that I am going there to prepare a place for you?"*

MSB: *"What makes my Father's house home, is your place in it. If this was not the ultimate conclusion of my mission, why would I even bother to do what I am about to do if it was not to prepare a place for you? I have come to persuade you of a place of seamless oneness where you belong."*

Awakening Truth: Jesus wasn't becoming a building contractor in heaven. In His death and resurrection, He prepared a place of restored intimate oneness—not a distant mansion but seamless union. The Father's house isn't where you're going someday; it's where you belong right now. Home isn't a location—it's your place in Him. There is more than enough space for everyone!

Reflection: What if "preparing a place" wasn't about constructing heavenly real estate but about restoring your awareness of belonging? The difference between slave and son is that the slave only works there—for the son, the Father's house is HOME. You're not working toward acceptance. You're not performing for a place. You belong. You're already home.

There is no place like home—in Him.

There is no place like heaven—within.

God is home in me.

Welcome home.

Appendix B
Gospel Scripture Unveiled

A Translation Comparison Study
Seeing the Awakening Gospel Through Two Lenses

Why Two Translations?

Throughout this appendix, we compare two translations:

NIV (New International Version): The most widely read modern translation. When the awakening message appears clearly in the NIV, it shows these truths have been hiding in plain sight all along.

MSB (Mirror Study Bible): Francois du Toit's translation with extensive Greek word studies, emphasizing union with Christ and identity restoration. Where MSB differs from NIV, we've noted the Greek basis for its reading.

The goal isn't to declare one translation "correct" and the other "wrong." It's to show what the Greek *can* support—dimensions often obscured by traditional renderings.

A Note on Greek Grammar
Understanding who you already are in Christ

Greek tenses emphasize *how* an action occurs, not just *when*. The **Perfect tense** describes a past completed action whose results continue into the present. When Paul writes that you "have been saved" (Ephesians 2:5, 8 NIV), he uses the Perfect Passive Participle—grammatically declaring that you ARE what you were MADE.

The awakening message isn't imported into the text; it's encoded in the grammar.

1. John 3:16–17 — "For God So Loved the World"
The most quoted verse in Scripture. But what if we've been reading it through a lens of conditional threat rather than unconditional belonging?

NIV: *"For God so loved the world that he gave his one and only Son, that whoever believes in him shall not perish but have eternal life. For God did not send his Son into the world to condemn the world, but to save the world through him."*

MSB: *"The entire cosmos is the object of God's affection. And he is not about to abandon his creation—the gift of his Son is for mankind to realize their origin in him who mirrors their authentic birth—begotten not of flesh but of the Father. In this persuasion the life of the ages echoes within the individual and announces that the days of regret and sense of lost-ness are over. God has no intention to condemn anyone—he has sent his Son, not as Judge, but as Savior of the world. The kosmos was rescued because of him!"*

Greek Insights

- **KOSMOS (κόσμος):** In the NT, kosmos refers to the *entire* human family—not a geography but a people. The entire human family is the object of God's affection.

- **APOLLUMI (ἀπόλλυμι):** The KJV translates this "perish." But it's the same word translated "lost" in Luke 15—the lost sheep, lost coin, lost son. Jesus' own usage establishes the meaning: you cannot be lost unless you *belong*. Apollumi also suggests a sense of uselessness—that which comes to ruin and amounts to nothing. The opposite of perishing isn't just surviving—it's awakening to your belonging.

- **DIDOMI (δίδωμι):** Traditionally "gave." But didomi can mean to give something to someone that already belongs to them—thus, to *return*. The gift of the Son is the return of what was always ours: our origin, our identity, our authentic birth.

- **MONOGENES (μονογενής):** "One and only" (NIV) or "only begotten." Begotten only by the Father and not of the flesh. Here's the awakening key: in Him we recognize our true beginning—as in the authentic original mold. See John 1:12–13.

- **ECHO (ἔχω):** Traditionally "have" (eternal life). But echō means to hold, to embrace—as in echo. The life of the ages isn't a future reward; it echoes within the individual *now*, announcing that the days of lost-ness are over.

- **PISTEUO (πιστεύω):** "Believes"—but pisteuo is persuasion, not intellectual agreement. In this persuasion the life of the ages echoes. Faith doesn't create the reality; it awakens you to the reality that was always there.

- **SOZO (σώζω) — v17:** "God has no intention to condemn anyone." The verb is Aorist Passive Subjunctive (σωθῇ)—*having been rescued*. Not "might be rescued someday" but a completed rescue announced in the present. The Son was sent not as Judge but as Savior of the kosmos.

→ *See Glossary: APOLLUMI, PISTEUO, ZOE, MONOGENES, KOSMOS, SOZO*

Awakening Insight

This isn't a verse about God's conditional offer—it's a verse about God's relentless pursuit. The entire human family belongs to Him. The Son wasn't sent to create belonging but to reveal it. You cannot be lost unless you were first found. The "eternal life" isn't a future destination—it's the life of the ages echoing within you right now, announcing that your days of lost-ness are over. And God's purpose was never condemnation—it was rescue. A rescue already accomplished.

Traditional Reading	Awakening Reading
"World" = sinful planet needing rescue	"Kosmos" = entire human family, object of affection
"Gave" = offered conditionally	"Gave" = returned what already belongs
"Believes" = intellectual decision to accept	"Persuasion" = awakening to what's already true
"Perish" = eternal punishment	"Lost" = living unaware of belonging (Luke 15)
"Eternal life" = future heavenly reward	"Life of the ages" = present reality echoing within
God sent Son to save from condemnation	God sent Son as Savior, not Judge—rescue already accomplished

2. John 8:21-24 — "Die in Your Sins"

Jesus confronts the Pharisees about identity—theirs and His.

NIV: *"I am going away, and you will look for me, and you will die in your sin. Where I go, you cannot come... if you do not believe that I am he, you will indeed die in your sins."*

MSB: *"Your belief-system keeps you trapped in blindfold-mode... your religion is a cul-de-sac... you are not convinced about who I am, you wouldn't know who you are."*

Greek Insights

- **Singular vs. plural:** "Sin" (v21) is singular (ἁμαρτία); "sins" (v24) is plural. Singular = root condition (distorted identity); plural = symptoms.

- **"I AM" (ἐγώ εἰμι / ego eimi):** The divine name from Exodus 3:14. NIV adds "he" in italics because it's not in the Greek. Jesus simply says "I AM."

- **The barrier:** MSB captures what the Greek implies—it's not divine prohibition but perception failure. "Your belief-system keeps you trapped."

→ *See Glossary: EGO EIMI, HAMARTIA*

Awakening Insight

Knowing who Jesus is reveals who you are. His identity unlocks yours. This isn't just Christology—it's anthropology.

Traditional Reading	Awakening Reading
"Sin" = generic sinfulness	"Sin" = distorted identity
Barrier is divine prohibition	Barrier is belief-system blindness
"I AM" = Christological claim only	"I AM" also reveals YOUR identity
"Die in sins" = eternal punishment	"Die in sins" = remain in death-consciousness

3. Ephesians 2:1-5 — "Dead in Trespasses and Sins"

The classic passage on human condition and divine rescue. But what kind of "death"? What kind of "rescue"?

NIV: *"As for you, you were dead in your transgressions and sins, in which you used to live when you followed the ways of this world... But because of his great love for us, God, who is rich in mercy, made us alive with Christ even when we were dead in transgressions—it is by grace you have been saved."*

MSB: *"Picture where God found us. We were in a death trap of an inferior lifestyle, constantly living below the blueprint measure of our lives... This is how grace rescued us: we were co-quickened together with Christ."*

Greek Insights

- **HAMARTIA (ἁμαρτία):** From ha (without) + meros (allotted form). Sin = living below your design specs, not just "doing bad things."
- **"Sons of disobedience":** Greek ἀπειθείας (apeitheia) = un-persuadedness, unbelief. Not rebellion—perception failure.
- **"Made alive" (συνεζωοποίησεν):** Aorist tense = completed past action. You WERE made alive. Done.
- **"You have been saved" (σεσωσμένοι):** Perfect Passive Participle = "you ARE what you were MADE." This is the grammatical key to awakening theology.

→ *See Glossary: HAMARTIA, SOZO, SUN- compounds*

Awakening Insight

We weren't bad people who became good. We were asleep people who were awakened. The Perfect Passive Participle declares present identity from past action: you ARE what you were MADE

Traditional Reading	Awakening Reading
"Dead in sins" = spiritual death from behavior	"Dead in sins" = death trap of living below design
"Disobedience" = willful rebellion	"Disobedience" = unbelief, un-persuadedness
"Made alive" = future resurrection hope	"Made alive" = past completed action
Grammar not emphasized	Perfect Passive Participle = present identity

4. Romans 2:4 — "His Kindness Leads to Repentance"

The subtitle of this book is "Restorative Metanoia." This verse shows what metanoia really means.

NIV: *"Or do you show contempt for the riches of his kindness, forbearance and patience, not realizing that God's kindness is intended to lead you to repentance?"*

MSB: *"Do not underestimate God's kindness. The wealth of his benevolence and his resolute refusal to let go of us, is because he continues to hear the echo of his likeness in us! Thus, his patient passion is to shepherd everyone into a radical mind shift."*

Greek Insights

- **METANOIA (μετάνοια):** *Meta* (together with/beyond) + *nous* (mind/perception). A radical shift in perception—NOT guilt-driven behavior change.
- **The Latin corruption**: Jerome translated *metanoia* as *paenitentia* (penance). "Penance" became "repentance" (re-penance). A Greek word meaning "transformation of perception" became a Latin word meaning "feel sorry and make up for it."
- **What causes metanoia**: Not guilt. Not fear. Not threat. *Kindness.* The revelation of God's goodness shifts perception.

→ *See Glossary: METANOIA (Most Essential Terms)*

Awakening Insight

It's the revelation of God's goodness that leads to metanoia—not our metanoia that leads God to goodness. Faith is not a decision; it is a discovery.

Traditional Reading	Awakening Reading
"Repentance" = feel sorry, change behavior	"Repentance" = radical mind shift, awakening
Caused by guilt and conviction	Caused by revelation of God's kindness
Faith = a decision to make	Faith = a discovery to experience

5. Ephesians 1:4-5 — "Chosen Before the Foundation"

When were you chosen? Before creation—or before the fall?

NIV: *"For he chose us in him before the creation of the world to be holy and blameless in his sight. In love he predestined us for adoption to sonship through Jesus Christ."*

MSB: *"He associated us in Christ before the fall of the world. Jesus is God's mind made up about us. He always knew in his love that he would present us again face-to-face before him in blameless innocence."*

Greek Insights

- **KATABOLE (καταβολή):** Standard lexicons translate this as "foundation." However, the verb kataballō can also mean "to throw down, cast down"—leading some scholars to read this as "before the fall of the world." Either way: God's choice preceded anything that could disqualify you.

- **KATENOPION (κατενώπιον):** "Face-to-face." The closest possible proximity. Not forgiven from a distance—presented face-to-face.

- **"In Christ" (ἐν Χριστῷ):** Paul's most frequent phrase. Your location determines your identity. You were placed IN Christ before you were placed in Adam.

→ *See Glossary: EN CHRISTŌ, HUIOTHESIA*

Awakening Insight

You were found in Christ before you were lost in Adam. God's choice preceded your failure. His love isn't reactive—it's original.

Traditional Reading	Awakening Reading
"Foundation" = before creation began	"Foundation" = before the FALL
"Chose" = election (Calvinist debate)	"Chose" = God's mind made up about us
Implication: some chosen, some not?	Found in Christ before lost in Adam
Result: will be holy someday	Presented face-to-face NOW

6. John 10:9-10 — "Life Abundantly"

Jesus' purpose statement. Who is the thief—and what does "abundant" really mean?

NIV: *"I am the gate; whoever enters through me will be saved. They will come in and go out, and find pasture. The thief comes only to steal and kill and destroy; I have come that they may have life, and have it to the full."*

MSB: *"I am the door and the sheep who enter because of who I am is safe to roam freely and find pasture. The thief shepherd has no other agenda but to steal, kill and he couldn't care less if he lost some sheep. I have come with the sole purpose for you to have life in its most complete form."*

Greek Insights

- **"I am the door" (ἐγώ εἰμι):** Another EGO EIMI statement. Jesus doesn't just show the way; He IS the way.
- **"Will be saved" (σωθήσεται):** From SOZO—rescue, heal, make whole. Not just "go to heaven when you die" but present wholeness, safety, freedom.
- **Context (John 9-10):** The "thief" refers to the Pharisees who just excommunicated the man born blind. Not generic thieves—religious leaders who steal identity and kill hope.
- **APOLLUMI (ἀπόλλυμι):** Often "destroy," but also "lose" (same word in Luke 15: lost sheep, lost coin, lost son). The thief-shepherd LOSES sheep through careless neglect.
- **PERISSOS (περισσός):** "Exceeding, abundant, more than sufficient." Life in its most complete form.

→ *See Glossary: ZOE, SOZO, EGO EIMI*

Awakening Insight

Jesus' sole purpose isn't sin management or behavior modification. It's LIFE—whole, full, complete, overflowing. The thief-shepherd doesn't just kill sheep—he loses them through religious carelessness.

Traditional Reading	Awakening Reading
"Saved" = go to heaven when you die	"Saved" = present wholeness, safety, freedom
"Thief" = Satan or generic enemy	"Thief" = false religious leaders
"Destroy" = kill/eliminate	"Destroy" = LOSE through neglect
"Abundantly" = more quantity	"Abundantly" = most complete form
Jesus' purpose = save from hell	Jesus' purpose = give LIFE

7. Romans 8:17 — "Co-Heirs with Christ"

Are we conditionally heirs—or certainly included? The Greek grammar settles it.

NIV: *"Now if we are children, then we are heirs—heirs of God and co-heirs with Christ, if indeed we share in his sufferings in order that we may also share in his glory."*

MSB: *"The fact that we are God's offspring, certainly also means that we are equal heirs of God. Not only is God our portion, but we are his. We are co-heirs in Christ. So, whatever we may suffer, at any time could never separate us from our inclusion in his sufferings."*

Greek Insights

- **EIPER (εἴπερ) with Indicative Mood**: This is crucial. When eiper ("if indeed") appears with the Indicative mood, it assumes the fact is true. Not "if maybe" but "since, as is the case."
- **SUN- prefix appears 3x:** sunklēronomoi (co-heirs), sunpaschōmen (co-suffer), sundoxasthōmen (co-glorified). The co-inclusion is relentless.
- **SUNDOXASTHOMEN (συνδοξασθῶμεν):** Aorist Passive Subjunctive = inevitable fulfillment. Glory participation is a given, not a maybe.
- **"We are His":** MSB catches what NIV misses: "Not only is God our portion, but we are his." You're not just receiving from God—you ARE God's inheritance.

→ *See Glossary: SUN- compounds, DOXA*

Awakening Insight

The "if" doesn't express doubt—it expresses certainty. And notice: "Not only is God our portion, but we are His." You're not just receiving from God—you ARE God's inheritance.

Traditional Reading	Awakening Reading
"If indeed" = conditional, must qualify	"If indeed" = certain, since we ARE included
Suffering = requirement to earn glory	Suffering = cannot separate us from inclusion
"Co-heirs" = we receive from God	"Co-heirs" = we ARE God's inheritance too
Glory = future hope if we qualify	Glory = inevitable fulfillment, already secured

8. 1 John 1:9 — "If We Confess Our Sins"

The foundation of Christian confession practice. But is it about informing God—or reminding yourself?

NIV: *"If we confess our sins, he is faithful and just and will forgive us our sins and purify us from all unrighteousness."*

MSB: *"Our conversation takes on a brand new dynamic when we take sides with what God believes about us. So, instead of telling God about the detail of your sin, you remind yourself about the detail of your redemption. God doesn't need the information, you do."*

Greek Insights

- **HOMOLOGEO (ὁμολογέω):** Homos (same) + logos (word). To "say the same word"—agree with God's assessment. Not inform Him of your failures, but align with His declaration about you.
- **APHIEMI (ἀφίημι):** Lexically: apo (away from) + hiēmi (to send). Forgiveness as releasing, sending away. Du Toit's interpretive rendering captures the theological implication: restored to your true identity.
- **Grammar**: Both "forgive" and "cleanse" are Aorist Subjunctive—definite outcomes from the action of confession.
- **Direction of information:** Traditional reading: you inform God. Awakening reading: you agree with what God already declared. "God doesn't need the information, you do."

→ *See Glossary: HOMOLOGEO, APHIEMI*

Awakening Insight

Confession isn't informing God of your failures—He already knows. It's agreeing with His word about your redemption. You're reminding YOURSELF of the truth.

Traditional Reading	Awakening Reading
"Confess" = tell God your sins	"Confess" = agree with God's word about you
Purpose = receive forgiveness	Purpose = remind yourself of redemption
Direction = you inform God	Direction = you agree with what God declared

The Pattern Revealed

After examining these seven passages, a consistent pattern emerges. The Greek New Testament supports the awakening gospel in ways that traditional translations often obscure.

The Traditional Framework:

- Sin-focus: Behavioral failure requiring behavioral correction
- Future-orientation: Salvation as where you go when you die
- Conditional language: "If" statements creating uncertainty
- Separation emphasis: God and humanity as distant
- Performance: Ongoing need to maintain right standing

The Awakening Reading:

- Identity-focus: Sin as living below your design
- Present-reality: Salvation as present awakening
- Certainty language: Greek grammar expressing certainty
- Union emphasis: Found in Christ before lost in Adam
- Rest: Confession as agreement, not performance

Summary: Traditional vs. Awakening

Scripture	Traditional	Awakening
John 8:21-24	Believe or face punishment	Know Jesus → know yourself
Ephesians 2:1-5	Dead in bad behavior	Death trap of living below design
Romans 2:4	Be sorry, change behavior	Mind-shift through kindness
Ephesians 1:4-5	Chosen before creation	Found before lost in Adam
John 10:9-10	Saved from hell	Given life in most complete form
Romans 8:17	Suffer to earn glory	Certainly co-heirs; nothing separates
1 John 1:9	Tell God your sins	Agree with God about redemption

The awakening gospel doesn't contradict traditional translations—it deepens them, returning to Greek meanings that centuries of Latin influence have obscured. The good news was always this good. We just couldn't see it.

Now you can.

Now that you've seen what the Greek says, the question arises: why haven't we heard this before? Appendix C tells that story.

Tetelestai. It is finished. Now live from it.

Appendix C
How Did We Miss This?

The Historical Journey from Greek to English

If the awakening message is really there in the Greek—if the tenses, the word studies, the grammar all support this more beautiful gospel—then why haven't we heard it before?

The answer isn't conspiracy. It's history. It's how language, power, and institutions work over time.

We weren't deceived. We inherited a translation.

Latin Buried the Greek

When Jerome translated the Bible into Latin (the Vulgate, around 400 AD), it became THE Bible for Western Christianity for over a thousand years. Greek—the original language of the New Testament—was effectively lost to the West.

One translation choice tells the whole story:

Jerome translated *metanoia* as *paenitentia*.

Paenitentia became "penance." "Penance" eventually became "repentance"—literally "re-penance," implying repeated acts of sorrow and atonement.

A Greek word meaning "transformation of perception" became a Latin word meaning "feel sorry and do something to make up for it."

That single translation choice shaped a millennium of Western spirituality.

Augustine's Greek Problem

Augustine of Hippo (354–430 AD) is arguably the most influential theologian in Western Christian history. His writings shaped Catholic, Reformed, and Evangelical theology for sixteen centuries.

Augustine didn't read Greek well. He worked primarily from Latin translations.

His theology of original sin, total depravity, and the *massa damnata* (the condemned mass of humanity) became Western orthodoxy. Meanwhile, the Eastern Church—still reading Greek—emphasized *theosis* (union with God), a more hopeful view of human nature, and salvation as healing rather than legal transaction.

Same New Testament. Different source languages. Different Christianities.

The Reformation: Breakthrough and Blind Spot

Martin Luther recovered justification by faith. He returned to the Greek texts. Revolutionary.

But the Reformers were reacting AGAINST Catholic works-righteousness. Their emphasis landed on forensic justification—a legal courtroom declaration—rather than participatory union. They kept the sin-focus. They just changed the solution.

The Greek text supports union theology. Paul uses *en Christō* ("in Christ") over 160 times. The *sun-* prefix (co-quickened, co-raised, co-seated) saturates his letters. But the Reformation debate was about HOW you get saved. The deeper question—WHAT salvation actually means—got bypassed.

The Reformers recovered grace. But they kept the anthropology of human wretchedness.

Translation Inertia

Once the King James Version (1611) established certain English renderings, they became sacred. "Repentance." "Wages of sin." "Dead in trespasses."

Later translations work within that tradition. Translation committees are inherently conservative. Legitimate Greek meanings can remain buried simply because they haven't been part of the tradition.

Ministers learn Greek in seminary, but within a theological tradition. The tenses are taught. The theological implications often aren't. When tradition and grammar conflict, tradition usually wins—not from dishonesty, but from the power of inherited frameworks.

The Eastern Church Never Lost It

Here's the irony: the Orthodox Church has been teaching *theosis*, union, and participatory salvation for two thousand years. They never stopped reading Greek. They never went through the Latin filter.

The word "orthodox" itself makes the point: *orthos* (correct) + *doxa* (glory/belief) = correct belief. The Eastern Church called themselves Orthodox because they believed they were preserving the original, uncorrupted faith.

When Francois du Toit writes about being "co-quickened, co-raised, co-seated" with Christ, Eastern Orthodox readers don't find it novel. It's what they've always taught.

The awakening message isn't heterodox (wrong belief). It's actually *more* orthodox than the Latin-filtered tradition many of us inherited. We're not departing from historic Christianity—we're returning to it.

Why It's Emerging Now

Greek tools are accessible. Strong's Concordance is on your phone. Interlinear Bibles are free online. You no longer need seminary training to check what the Greek actually says.

The internet routes around gatekeepers. Teachers like Francois du Toit can publish without denominational approval.

Post-evangelical exhaustion. Millions have burned out on performance Christianity. They're asking: "Is this really the good news?"

East meets West. Orthodox theology is reaching Protestant audiences for the first time.

The Hope

The tragedy is real: Millions of sincere believers have spent their lives in guilt and religious performance—when the Greek text proclaims their completed inclusion in Christ.

But the hope is equally real: **The text hasn't changed.**

The treasures were buried, not destroyed. Every Greek New Testament still contains *metanoia*. Every manuscript still records Paul's perfect passive participles. The evidence waits for anyone willing to look.

We're not inventing a new gospel. We're recovering an ancient one.

The Latin said: *Paenitentia.* Do penance. Feel sorry. Try harder.
The Greek said: *Metanoia.* Change your mind. See differently. Wake up.
Two words. Two gospels. Two thousand years of difference.
Now you know which one was original.

With the history understood, we can now state the recovered gospel clearly. That's Appendix D.

Tetelestai. It is finished. Now live from it.

Appendix D
The Gospel of Awakening

Not becoming something new—waking up to who you've always been

You've studied the Greek words. You've seen how translation choices reveal or obscure the original meanings. You've learned why the Western church lost sight of these treasures.

Now it's time to answer the question: What IS the gospel when you put it all together?

This isn't new theology. It's ancient truth recovered.

The Good Announcement

The Greek word for "gospel" is *euangelion*—literally, "good announcement." Not good advice. Not good requirements. Good news about something that's already true.

What if the gospel is bigger than sin management? What if it's not just about where you go when you die, but about waking up to who you really are right now?

---

1. DESIGNED — You Were Chosen Before the Fall

Before you took your first breath, before the foundation of the world—God had you in mind.

> *"He chose us in him before the creation of the world to be holy and blameless in his sight."*
> — Ephesians 1:4 NIV

The Greek word *katabole* can mean "foundation" or "falling down." Either way: God chose you before there was anything to disqualify you.

You were found in Christ before you were lost in Adam.

2. DECEIVED — You Forgot Who You Were

Something went wrong. Not with God's design, but with our perception of it. We believed a lie about ourselves.

The Greek word *hamartia* (sin) suggests living without your allotted form—below your design specs.

> *"You were dead in your trespasses and sins..."*
> — Ephesians 2:1 NIV

Sin isn't just doing bad things. It's living below your design.

And here is what makes that even more stunning: sin entered a story where its defeat was already written. The

THE AWAKENING GLOSSARY

Lamb was slain before the foundation of the world (Revelation 13:8 NIV). God's mind was made up about us before creation began (Ephesians 1:4 NIV). Identity amnesia entered a universe where union was already the bedrock reality — and where the remedy was already accomplished before the problem fully unfolded.

We didn't become bad people who need to become good. We became asleep people who need to wake up.

3. DEMONSTRATED — Jesus Came to Wake You Up

Jesus came to reveal who God really is—and who you really are.

> *"I have come that they may have life, and have it to the full."*
> — John 10:10 NIV

On the cross, Jesus declared *"Tetelestai"*—"It is finished." The Greek perfect tense means completed action with permanent results.

Knowing who Jesus is reveals who you are. His identity unlocks yours.

Jesus was not God's emergency response plan. God's mind was made up before the foundation of the world. Jesus came not to rescue us from a burning hell that was never in the Greek — but to reveal what was always true: you were never outside Him. The gospel was never an evacuation plan. It was always an awakening.

4. DISCOVERED — The Response Is Awakening, Not Achievement

The Greek word *metanoia*—usually translated "repentance"—means a radical shift in perception. Seeing what you couldn't see before.

> *"God's kindness is intended to lead you to repentance."*
> — Romans 2:4 NIV

It's God's kindness—not guilt, not fear—that leads to this mind-shift.

Repentance isn't behavior modification. It's a mind-shift. Faith isn't a decision; it's a discovery.

5. DECLARED — You Are Already Included

The work is already done. You're not trying to get into Christ—you're waking up to the fact that you've been in Christ since before creation.

NIV: *"Made us alive with Christ even when we were dead in transgressions—it is by grace you have been saved."*

MSB: *"This happened while we were still dead in our trespasses and sins. God co-quickened us together with Christ—grace has saved you!"*

The Greek grammar (perfect passive participle) means "you ARE what you were MADE."

> *"God was reconciling the world to himself in Christ, not counting people's sins against them."*
> — 2 Corinthians 5:19 NIV

Written 25 years after the cross, Paul announces accomplished fact—not future possibility. *Reconciled*—past tense. *The world*—not just believers. *Not counting sins*—already.

You don't become a child of God. You wake up to discover you always were.

The early church had a word for what this inclusion actually means: theosis. Participation in divine life. Not forgiveness offered from a distance — restoration to your original design as a partaker of the divine nature (2 Peter 1:4 NIV). For the first thousand years of Christianity, before Jerome's Latin translation buried it, this was the gospel. Not rescue from wrath. Awakening into union. The Word became flesh so that flesh might be transfused with the Divine — and you were always the destination of that movement.

6. DEFINED — Live From Identity, Not For Identity

The awakened life isn't about trying harder. It's about living from the goodness that's already yours in Christ.

You don't obey to earn love—you obey because you've experienced it. You don't confess to maintain standing—you confess to remind yourself of your standing.

And where are you living from? Not from performance. Not from striving. From the perichoresis — the eternal exchange of love between Father, Son, and Spirit — into which you have been drawn and in which you have always belonged. Jesus declared it: "I am in my Father, and you are in me, and I am in you" (John 14:20 NIV). You were always the destination of that love. You are not outside looking in. You are home.

Religion says: Do this and become. The Gospel says: You already are—now live like it.

THE INVITATION

The gospel isn't an invitation to try harder at religion. It's an invitation to wake up.

"Wake up, sleeper, rise from the dead, and Christ will shine on you."
— Ephesians 5:14 NIV

At a Glance: The Six Points

1. **DESIGNED:** You were chosen in Christ before the fall. God's love is original, not reactive.

2. **DECEIVED:** Sin is living below your design, forgetting who you were made to be.

3. **DEMONSTRATED:** Jesus reveals the Father's heart and your true identity.

4. **DISCOVERED:** Repentance is a mind-shift. Faith is discovery, not decision.

5. **DECLARED:** You have been saved. You ARE what you were MADE.

6. **DEFINED:** Live FROM your identity, not FOR an identity you're trying to earn.

Traditional Gospel:	You are a sinner. Believe and you will be saved.
Awakening Gospel:	You are God's beloved. Wake up to who you've always been.

This is the Gospel of Awakening.

This is your invitation to come home to yourself.

A Final Word

I leave you with these words from Francois du Toit, whose Mirror Study Bible has informed so much of this journey:

"I dare you to begin to see everyone through love's eyes and stop putting them in little boxes of 'believers' and 'unbelievers' or whatever labels we've adopted—and witness the adventure of good news finding feet and voice and hands and heart in you!

What an opportunity for a great reconciliation to manifest through ordinary people living in the faith of Jesus Christ—and not in your efforts to defend your personal beliefs and policies! I echo Paul's prayer, for the eyes of your hearts to be flooded with light and that you may know, with fresh understanding, the fathomless love of Christ ignited in you!"

— Francois du Toit *(2 Corinthians 5:16, Acts 10:28, Ephesians 1:18)*

This is awakening theology with skin on. Not a doctrine to defend but a love to embody. Not boxes to sort people into but eyes to see them with.

The Greek has done its work. The history has been told. The gospel has been named.

Now go live it.

Tetelestai. It is finished. Now live from it.

Welcome to your new vocabulary.

Welcome to your new reality.

Welcome home.

Your Daily Awakening Practice

Morning Meditation: Choose one scripture from this list each day. Read it slowly three times. Close your eyes and ask the Holy Spirit: *"What does this reveal about who I already am?"*

Let the truth sink past your mind into your heart. Don't try to make it true—simply recognize what IS true.

Throughout the Day: Carry that truth with you. When doubt whispers, return to it. When fear rises, declare it. When religion tries to make you strive, remember: it's already finished.

Evening Reflection: Before sleep, reflect: *"How did this truth change how I saw myself today? Where did I live FROM it rather than FOR it?"*

Awakening Through Music

Truth doesn't only come through written words. Some of the most powerful awakening happens through music that bypasses the mind and speaks directly to the heart.

Few worship artists capture the essence of the beautiful gospel. These two are rare exceptions:

Rachel Cannon — Her songs don't beg for God's attention; they rest in His embrace. This is worship from union, not toward it. Listening to her is less performance and more encounter— music that carries the frequency of the beautiful gospel.

John Mark Pantana — His worship declares finished work and beloved identity. Songs that announce who you already are rather than who you're trying to become. Music for those awakening to what has always been true—that you were never outside the Father's embrace.

If the written word has begun your awakening, let these voices carry it deeper. Sometimes a single song accomplishes what a thousand pages cannot.

COMPLETE IN HIM: THE INCARNATION
The Capstone of Awakening

"In him, all the fullness of Deity resides in a human body. He proves that human life is tailor-made for God."
— Colossians 2:9 (MSB)

"We are complete in him. Jesus mirrors our wholeness and endorses our true identity. He is I AM in us."
— Colossians 2:10 (MSB)

The Revolutionary Truth:

The incarnation proves something stunning: **human life is tailor-made for God.**
Not tolerated. Not endured. *Tailor-made.* When Deity filled human flesh, it wasn't a compromise—it was a homecoming.
Jesus didn't come to show us how far we've fallen. He came to show us what we've always been.

The Shift:
- **Old:** I must become something I'm not
- **New:** I am awakening to what I've always been

In Practice: Stop trying to get God into you—He's already there. Stop trying to become complete—you already are.

The Awakening Gospel in One Declaration

I am not becoming something new—I am awakening to who I've always been in Christ. Chosen before creation, already seated in heavenly places, one spirit with Him, living and moving in Him, with nothing to earn and everything to realize. The work is finished. My identity is secure. I am awakening!

"The Moment You Realize"

*The moment you realize you were never separated... The moment you understand sin was only blindness... The moment you see that you've always been En Christo... The moment you know that religion was managing an illusion... The moment you discover the Father never turned His face away...
That's not the moment you become free. That's the moment you realize you always were.*

NOW WHAT?

You've reached the end of this glossary. But this isn't a conclusion — it's an ignition point.

The Greek has done its work. Something has shifted. And here's what I've learned: once this shift happens, it keeps happening. Every time you open Scripture with these eyes, you'll see something you missed before. The Bible you thought you knew becomes a love letter you're reading for the first time.

The words you just studied were never just definitions. They were veils being lifted. Aletheia arriving. And what you're awakening to is the same thing the declaration at the beginning named: we began in Christ. The union was never broken. You were always home.

Once you see it, you cannot unsee it.

Go Back

Take your most familiar verse — the one you've quoted a hundred times. Now read it through what you've learned here.

Let *metanoia* be restored perception, not guilt. Let *hamartia* be identity amnesia, not moral crime. Let *tetelestai* be the final word it actually is. Where Paul writes "if," hear "since." Where you read "faith," receive it — God's own faithfulness, already alive in you.

Something will open that was always there, waiting.

The text hasn't changed. You have.

Go Deeper

This glossary is a companion to a larger journey — one that was lived before it was written. Each book in The Awakening Series documents a real stage of revelation. Enter at any point:

More Than Gold — Where the journey begins — the traditional gospel, honestly held.

As in Heaven: Living in God's Kingdom Now — The Kingdom is present reality, not future hope.

Ascension — Seated with Christ in heavenly places — your current, actual position.

Awakening: Restorative Metanoia — The Greek opens everything. The beauty of the gospel, fully unveiled.

The Awakening Glossary: Companion Resource — The language of awakening — distilled and portable for daily use, small groups, and conferences.

Heavenly Health Hacks: God's Design for Vibrant Living — *Coming Soon* — Your body is the temple of the Holy Spirit, and caring for it is an act of worship. Food is a celebration of life, designed by a God who invented flavor, abundance, and the joy of a shared table. Health — on earth as it is in heaven.

Living Awakened: Coming Soon — *Walking it all out daily.*

All books are available free at M46Ministries.com. For those who want a hard copy, they are on Amazon at the lowest price the platform allows — because the goal is to get this into as many hands as possible, as simply as possible.

Go Remember

This isn't an invitation to try harder at religion. It's an invitation to wake up to what is already yours — to what has always been true.

Your soul already knows these things. That recognition — that yes, this is what I always sensed but couldn't name — that's not you learning something new. That's you remembering.

You were never a surprise to God. You have never been known differently than you are known right now. You were found in Christ before you were lost in Adam. You were loved before you were born.

We don't live toward the finished work. We live from it.

That's the difference between gift language and reward language — and it changes everything. Religion says do this, receive that. The beautiful gospel says it's already given. Wake up to it.

That shift has a signature. It feels like joy that doesn't need permission — not an emotion that rises and falls with circumstances, but a settled state, because joy is a Person and union with Him is unbreakable. It feels like rest — not laziness, but the deep exhale of someone who has stopped carrying what was never theirs to carry, who has finally come home. And it feels like hope that has moved from fragile to certain — no longer wishful thinking about a future outcome, but confident expectation rooted in something already finished. These aren't feelings you work up. They're what awakening produces when the striving stops.

This is your awakening. This is your remembering.

Tetelestai. It is finished. Now live from it.
Welcome home. The cage is open. Fly.

—Bryan

ABOUT BRYAN ELLIOTT

Bryan Elliott approaches everything the way an engineer would — layer by layer, asking: if this is true, what does that mean? And if that's true, what changes?

Applied to theology, that process led somewhere he never expected: to Greek words hiding in plain sight for centuries, to Church Fathers who understood a gospel the Western church had largely forgotten, and to a God so much better than religion had described that it felt almost too good to be true.

It wasn't.

Bryan is a professional engineer, serial entrepreneur, and holder of multiple technological patents — bringing the same systematic, layer-by-layer innovation to both the marketplace and the Kingdom. He is founder and CEO of Flō Energy Solutions Inc., operating across North America, and sits on numerous boards and advisory boards spanning corporate and charitable sectors.

He co-founded M46 Ministries alongside his daughter Bryn to freely share the revelation of the Father's heart — because what was freely given should be freely shared. He co-founded Bee Me Kidz, a charity bringing restoration to children and families across multiple cities. As a speaker and podcaster, Bryan carries this message of awakening to conferences, gatherings, and audiences hungry for a gospel bigger than religion handed them.

He and his wife Teresa live in New Brunswick, Canada, where together they are raising a beautiful family — four girls and two boys, with their beloved daughter Abbe cheering them on from heaven. Teresa brings over 30 years of ministry experience, including 20 years as a senior pastor, and now co-labours with Bryan in M46 Ministries — carrying this same revelation of the Father's heart together. Their story is one of the most powerful testaments to the gospel of restoration you will read. You can find it at M46Ministries.com/marriage-redemption.

Despite the breadth of what he's involved in, writing now occupies the majority of Bryan's time — and that's not by accident. God has repositioned him with a remarkable level of freedom and flexibility to do exactly this: to write, to dig, and to share what he finds. For someone wired to build things, the greatest adventure turned out to be building in words — with Him.

THE AWAKENING SERIES

The Awakening Series — More Than Gold, As in Heaven, Ascension, Awakening: Restorative Metanoia, The Awakening Glossary, and the forthcoming Heavenly Health Hacks and Living Awakened — is one man's journey of awakening, documented in real time. Not a curriculum. Each of us walks our own unique path of remembering. The hope is simply that this journey inspires and accelerates yours.

This glossary is the companion resource to the entire series — and a standalone resource for personal study, small groups, and conferences. The Mirror Study Bible (MSB) by Francois du Toit, whose foreword graces the Awakening book, has been a foundational reference throughout this journey, has been a foundational reference throughout this journey.

**All books free at M46Ministries.com
Hard copies on Amazon at the lowest price the platform allows**

Bryan & Teresa Elliott — New Brunswick, Canada

"Wake up, sleeper, rise from the dead, and Christ will shine on you."
— Ephesians 5:14 (NIV)